PASSAGE INTO SPIRIT

Books by John-Roger

Awakening Into Light
Divine Essence
Blessings of Light
Disciples of Christ
Dream Voyages
Forgiveness: The Key to the Kingdom
God Is Your Partner
Inner Worlds of Meditation
The Journey of a Soul
Loving Each Day
Loving Each Day for Moms & Dads
Loving Each Day for Peacemakers
Manual on Using the Light
Momentum: Letting Love Lead (with Paul Kaye)
The Path to Mastership
Psychic Protection
The Power Within You
Relationships: Love, Marriage & Spirit
Sex, Spirit, and You
The Spiritual Family
Spiritual High
The Spiritual Promise
Spiritual Warrior: The Art of Spiritual Living
The Tao of Spirit
Walking with the Lord
The Way Out Book
Wealth & Higher Consciousness
What's It Like Being You? (with Paul Kaye)
When Are You Coming Home? (with Pauli Sanderson)

For further information, please contact:
MSIA®
P. O. Box 513935
Los Angeles, CA 90051-1935
www.msia.org

PASSAGE INTO SPIRIT

John-Roger

Edited by Rick Edelstein-Matisse

Published by Mandeville Press
P. O. Box 513935
Los Angeles, California 90051-1935
323/737-4055
www.mandevillepress.org
jrbooks@msia.org

Printed in the United States of America
ISBN 0-914829-25-4

Dedication

Once in a while, someone comes along who is an inspiration. This is often because of something they have done, something they have added, or even something they are going to do. Of course, this individual qualifies on all of these.

There are, however, those *rare* individuals who add *that* something special just because of who they are. To this *rare individual*, I have the utmost pleasure of dedicating this book. Alas, I flounder for words to convey the thanks from this dedicated heart to another heart *just as dedicated*. Perhaps it will be sufficient just to say, "Thank you."

To John Morton

Contents

Acknowledgements

Many months ago, John Morton started asking me questions about passing through the realms of Light. I replied that the answers were to be found in the material I had given over the years and that *his* answers could also be found there. He said okay and started searching. It soon became obvious to me, given John's other work, that this project could involve more than one person. Nevertheless, he continued with it as though he alone were to dig out the answers from the mass of information made available to him.

Soon, and much to his credit, John started asking others to participate with him on this project. Now I would like to acknowledge those people for giving of their time in countless hours and effort to making this book available: Stede Barber, production and design; Betsy Alexander, copy editing; Theresa Hocking, glossary and index; Ingrid Avallon, design consultant; Vivien Smith and Maggie Stuhl, production assistants; Holly Duggan and Kathleen Safron, editorial assistants.

Introduction

A child once asked me, "Why do I have to die?" Perhaps the child in each of us wonders about that. Allow me to share the conversation I had with that dear child.

"No, you don't have to die. Just your body."

"Why?"

"Because it's designed that way."

"Why can't I live forever?"

"You do. It's called the Soul. You are the Soul that *does* live forever."

"Then why do I have to come here in a body?"

"You're just here to have experiences, to learn."

"Like in school?"

"Yes."

"And then I graduate?"

"Exactly."

"When I graduate then I'm forever again?"

"You got it!"

And a little child shall lead them.[1]

---

1. Isaiah 11:6, Revised Standard Version

In essence, that conversation defines the reason for and the process of planet-Earth incarnation for each of the great number of Souls experiencing this world. The mind and ego demand more information in order to understand and accept the concept, however. This book offers such information. I suggest to you, though, that the mind and ego are the enemies of the Soul, so I am doubtful that intellectual understanding alone will create acceptance.

The true acceptance is on a level for which there are no words. I offer the words only for that part of your makeup that wants to understand mentally. If—with all the words—you still don't get it, I then offer the essence and experience of Spirit. This energy weaves in and out, above and below, and all around the words. Some people listen. Others actually hear. In order to get the essence of the way Spirit works, you have to do both. Listen with the ears of the experienced adult. Hear with the purity of the child.

Why Are We Here?
(Or Are We?)

First there is Spirit,
and out of Spirit comes God.

Spirit totally encompasses every level in every universe from eternity to eternity, from infinity to infinity. The Soul is the extension out of Spirit. The most experienced Soul *is* God.

The Soul of a human being is individualized energy that has the ability to experience the levels of Spirit. It just does not have all the experiences, which is why the Soul incarnates to levels below God.

Before you are born, the Soul and the high self (see the section on the high self) go before what we call the karmic board, and the lords of the akashic records share information. (The information is not in a language you would understand on the physical level.) The akashic board has every experience, every emotion, every action, every incompleted action, every promise, every every, of all your previous existences. The akashic "computer" is beyond description. Suffice it to say that all information about you is available. The akashic board then presents the choices to your high self and Soul. To translate their approach to an almost prosaic level, they might say, "Soul, here are all the bags you have around you of things you did not finish in your worlds. Now there is a chance for you to work it out, in this incarnation, or you can do just a little at a time."

You see, some of you have created such heavy karma from previous lifetimes, that you may, in that meeting, choose not to balance all of it in one more lifetime (although many of you who are reading this now have chosen to clean up your karma this last time and join the God-realms). Whether you do it or not is where free will (or free won't) comes in. The keepers of the akashic records do not care or judge. They just offer the information.

Once your Soul and high self make the choice, they blueprint your entire life in order to create the maximum opportunity for you to fulfill the karma you have chosen to complete. This includes your mother, father, place of birth, gender, physical makeup (including any handicaps), and so on. So the next time you find yourself complaining about your physical condition, a relative, or the way society relates to your gender or race, know that all that information was totally accessible when you made your highest choices for this incarnation, the highest choices being those that would balance karma.

Know that each situation and circumstance serves you as a stepping-stone into Spirit, chosen specifically with that intention. It has all been predetermined on the Soul level. If, like so many people, you hide behind the veil of forgetfulness with your feet stuck in ego, those same circumstances will be painful obstacles. It doesn't have to be that way. It's your choice. Any situation can be either information that leads you more directly to the heart of God or a painful lesson that may make the return home a little longer. Regardless of the choice, not one Soul will be lost. It's simply that some people may take ten or ten thousand more existences to learn from experiences.

The Process of Incarnation

As the Soul incarnates down into this world, it picks up an etheric body (sheath), which is a very fine substance that covers the Soul. As the Soul continues to descend, it picks up a mental, a causal, and an astral body (sheath). Then you are born. Birthing is the act of picking up the physical body.

As an infant, you are provided with a veil of forgetfulness. This is a spiritual device that is part of the equipment of incarnation. If you were consciously aware of the karmic lessons and balancing actions of this lifetime, you might try to avoid some, dismiss others, and handle others with a habitual response. In order that you approach each experience as a new opportunity on this divine learning mission, the veil of forgetfulness descends, usually by the time you are seven to eight years of age.

The levels of communication, established in Spirit, continue even after you are born, but your conscious self may be unaware of them, unaware, that is, until you practice a process of inner attunement (see the section on spiritual exercises).

Each level of existence is run by the level above it. The level above it is almost like a magnet, attracting you to ascend and participate on a higher plane. It is similar to working in a large organization; the better you handle the work in the position you are holding, the greater the opportunities for advancement and promotion. Such is the case in Spirit. The physical is run by the astral; the astral, by the causal; the causal, by the mental; the mental, by the etheric; and the etheric, by the Soul. The Soul is run by God.

By levels of existence I don't mean levels that are like stories in a building. Rather, look at them as vibration rates. All the vibrations are occurring simultaneously. As the vibrations "thin" themselves out, the sounds and colors of each vibration frequency become defined.

Who we are is brighter than all the lower levels, brighter even than the Lords of these levels. We are magnificent, but the physical body stops us from truly seeing our magnificence because we're trained to look out here, externally, at and through the body of flesh. It is only through attunement, when we turn inward, that we can truly see what is truly there.

Is There Anything
Below the
Physical Realm?

As there are levels above the physical realm, including our true home, the Soul realm, so are there lower levels below this physical realm. These areas, descending from the physical, greatly influence the way we fulfill, or avoid, our karmic destiny.

The subconscious is the part that retains what we forget on the conscious level; the information is still available, for the subconscious stores it until you are ready to call it forward. What slipped out of your consciousness can be profound and creative, or it may be as picayune as where you put your sunglasses (which are sitting on the top of your head).

The subconscious is a valuable level of energy. It is particularly useful at those times when a part of you (the basic self) chooses to forget an intended task or information that requires action. The memory of the incomplete actions rests in the subconscious. Sometimes the awareness of the incompletions will come to the conscious self just by calling on it. At other times, it will only rise when you (the basic and conscious selves) are distracted or relaxed, and then the awareness will often come present on the energy of a forgotten item.

Just below the subconscious is the unconscious level, the level that is unknown. In this level are all the things we have taken from the spiritual and pushed down through the physical into the subconscious and the unconscious. Then we say we are finished with them. There are no false

endings in Spirit. Spirit's eternal nature holds until completion occurs—and beyond that. With completion, the
undone things, the imbalanced emotions, and the unkind
acts are balanced by doing, loving, and caring.

You can self-righteously declare that you are finished
with someone or something, but the you that is inside you
knows better. That you that knows is the completer, the
essence of Spirit, the Mystical Traveler within you (see the
section on the Mystical Traveler). Even though you have
powerfully pushed those karmic opportunities down into
the unconscious, it is precisely there that they wait. In the
unconscious they wait. Spirit has infinite patience, lasting
through eternity and back.

The unconscious has finite patience. This means that the
unconscious will provoke you to deal with the karma this
lifetime. Sometimes the karmic reminders come up simply
as thoughts; at other times, as constipation (of mind and
bowels). If you don't listen, they may also create asthma or
even cancer. The closer to the end of the finite patience of
the unconscious, the more extreme will be the messages,
and they all say the same thing: "Hey, listen! Stop your denial. Stop your self-righteous declarations of being right.
Stop stopping your spiritual progress, and listen!"

For those who do listen, Spirit is available in the twink-
ling of an eye. Sometimes the eye of the ego is huge, so
the total twinkle may take a little while. I suggest you
don't ignore the early signals from your unconscious. If
you do, your karma may surface 20 years from now in
a more drastic form. Tapping into the unconscious (the
storehouse of incomplete actions) can be a spiritual bless-
ing, for it allows you to be aware of and complete your
karma and then return home, to God.

Below the unconscious are habits and addictions.
(These may be above, also; it depends on the behavior.)

People have been involved in behavior patterns for so long (e.g., biting nails, biting hangnails, smoking, etc.) that they're no longer aware of what they are doing. For example, a person might smoke while talking on the phone. They reach in their pocket for their cigarette pack, but there is no cigarette pack. A few minutes later they may reach in the same pocket again because of habit and addiction, totally unaware that they just did that. It's a habit based on addiction. The pack is always in the same pocket, the addiction says to reach, and the hand habitually goes for the pocket.

Below this level are what we call obsessions and compulsions. In *Macbeth*, Lady Macbeth walks around, rubbing her hands and saying, "Out, damned spot! Out, I say!" That is obsessive behavior. She took part in the murder of the former king, so awake or sleepwalking, she is obsessed with getting her hands clean of the supposed spot, symbolic of the murder.

Most sleepwalking comes out of this area of obsessions and compulsions. People can walk around with their eyes open but their mind asleep. Many youngsters will sleepwalk. Some do it in their minds, thinking they are going into the bathroom to urinate, and they wet the bed.

Compulsions and obsessions are related to and yet deeper than habits and general addictive behavior. Kleptomaniacs, narcotic addicts, and alcoholics fall into these areas.

Entities

Below compulsions are possessions, which are usually disincarnate entities. An entity cannot take over a body unless an individual abandons the body through involvement in addictive, obsessive, or compulsive patterns. Suicide attempts also open the body to possession by an entity. The entity has the right to take over the body. The person is not dead. It's just that they are pushed back. The entity that has taken over the body might like alcohol, so the person starts drinking. That is a possession.

An entity can be removed, but if you take it off a person and they still don't change their behavior, a new entity can come in. In this situation, you have to educate the physical person who is in there, along with the entity. The entity will not want to listen because it is running the body, but it does not own the body. If the entity doesn't leave the body, the person has somebody else running them. This is similar to some marriages, where the husband or wife determines what the spouse does. This, however, is often done out of love.

Possessions don't operate from the area of love. They are going to use the person to their own advantage. It is justified, in a way, because the person gave up responsibility to his or her body and allowed the entity to enter. The entity does not get any excess karma for doing that, but the person does—for giving up responsibility for his or her physical body.

Depending on the evolution of the entity, it can live on any of these levels: subconscious, unconscious, obsessive, compulsive, or possessive. These levels are in each of us, and the entity comes in on the level that is accessible.

The entity could come from the astral, causal, mental, or etheric realm. Most mediums tell you that their guides, which are possessions and entities, come from the causal, mental, or etheric level. They call them masters, ascended masters, and the Great White Brotherhood. Occasionally, some entities can give you good advice. Check it out. If the information contributes to your joy, health, and abundance, you might choose to follow what the guide tells you. To ensure that the suggested direction will contribute to your highest good, I suggest that you check out the advice each time before acting on the guide's direction.

Sometimes entities are very smart; sometimes, quite stupid. Sometimes they take over familiar forms and misrepresent themselves to be your Uncle Charles, for example, when they are actually just using information you released in the personality form and astral level. An entity may also be a personality projection coming out of the unconscious or astral realm. Uncle Charles may have evolved to higher levels, while the entity hangs out around you in the form of Uncle Charles. Some other energies have taken over that form and say they are Uncle Charles, but they are deceivers.

Yes, entities may very well be liars, which is another good reason to check out anything you think you hear or are directed to do from the inner levels. Just because they (or some fortune-teller) may have certain relevant facts about Uncle Charles (or your past), this doesn't mean they know any more than you do about the intended direction of your life. Check it out before you check out.

An entity, as defined in the dictionary, is a being having self-contained existence. Therefore, all Souls are entities, but not all entities have Souls.

Basic Self, Conscious Self, and High Self

Below the obsessions is what is known as the basic self. The basic self is the one that opens and closes the psychic centers of the body and the one that maintains the body. It is the child within each of us. As an energy form, it is physically located in the stomach area. The basic self may often be in conflict with the aware part of you of the physical level, which we call the conscious self. Above the conscious self, between the etheric body and the cosmic mirror, sits a high self, although the high self can be from any realm (astral, causal, mental, or etheric). The physical location of the high self is usually above the head.

The high self gives all the karmic directions for everything below it, but it has no control over the Soul. The Soul is perfect. Everything below it is imperfect. There is usually something incomplete below the Soul.

For the most part, the basic self talks to the high self throughout your lifetime. It might say, "What are we to do in this lifetime?" If the basic got into trouble because it participated in an action that was not supportive of the divine path chosen in Soul, it might say to the high self, "What do we do now?" The high self might just respond, "What do you mean 'we,' basic? You got yourself into this mess, creating more karma than originally intended. I'll just observe until you and lazy conscious self over there come back to the divine path we agreed upon with Soul."

The basic self (or selves; sometimes there is more than one) and the high self (usually only one) communicate with each other. The basic self also communicates directly with the conscious self. In order to do this, the basic has to go through possessions, compulsions, obsessions, and addictions (if any) and unconscious and subconscious levels just to get to the conscious self on the physical level. Similarly, the conscious self and high self have to go through the same process before they can communicate with the basic self and point it toward a responsible direction.

The basic might stop short and get or give mixed directions. Use your awareness and activate the conscious self. Consciously, always check out a direction. In other words, look before you leap. In this case, however, look inside, where the inner truth is known.

You can often recognize when a person is acting from the basic self, for they generally express through an emotional pattern. In that way the basic can be seen. The conscious self can be seen because here we are, in the physical sense; here and now is the conscious self's domain when it claims it. The high self is not to be seen with normal or even highly perceptive physical vision, but it can be contacted when the inner vision is sufficiently attuned.

The basic will often relate to human laws through the guilt that might be provoked by disobeying the rules of the game. These can be such things as the parents' guidelines, the teacher's rules, a traffic stop-sign, tax regulations, the social mores regarding fidelity, and your own high self's ethics. As soon as you feel guilt, you can bet that your basic is involved.

When Jesus said, "I and the Father are one,"[2] he was saying that "the Father" is the high self and the "I" is the conscious self. When he said, "I am the way, and the truth, and the life,"[3] he was then talking from the high self. Keep in mind, however, that although the high self is our God-source connection, it is not in Soul, not in the positive realms of God. The high self and the karmic board—as high as they are—both dwell in the lesser realms.

2. John 10:30, Revised Standard Version
3. John 14:6, Revised Standard Version

The high self exists within all the lower realms in order to be available to guide the karmic plan on each particular level. The Soul knows what the plan is, but it is the high self's responsibility to be the caretaker for the karmic indicators on the lower levels. These indicators are the joy or lack of joy in your life, the health or dis-ease in your life, the care and grace or accident-prone expressions in your life.

Here's how it may have worked before your recent embodiment onto this karmic planet. At a particular time—and it could be 200 years before your physical birth—the karmic board checks with the Soul and goes over those things you have to learn in order to come home to the Soul level once and for all. The high self and the basic self are chosen to support the plan. The basic self, the Soul, and the high self look at the master plan for life and agree upon the blueprints for your life, which are worked out to fit a matrix that includes all your DNA and RNA propensities and the optimum opportunities to balance the karma. This is not predestined. This is where free will comes in.

Look at your life right now. Look at the choices you exercise. Are they all in support of health, wealth, and happiness? Are they all in support of unconditional loving and no judgment? If they're not, you are not yet cooperating with the opportunities of your divine plan. If I were a salesman, I'd pitch these as "Opportunities for a Lifetime!" Or, if you blow it, "Opportunities for Many More Lifetimes."

The high self, Soul, and basic self are likely to come forward at a particular time and meet with your intended mother's and father's Souls, high selves, and basic selves and those of any intended brothers and sisters. During all this, where is the conscious self? This energy extends out of Soul as unconditioned energy. It usually awakens at birth and has its most intensive training up to approximately three years of age. This training continues until the physical body is about seven or eight years old.

When your parents have sexual intercourse and conception takes place, the basic self will enter the body within 24 hours. Using the matrix provided by the genetic code, the basic self starts formulating what we call a baby. During gestation, the baby will first be female. If the baby is to be a boy, the male genital organs will appear later.

When the basic comes in, it has knowledge of the entire plan, and it builds according to that design. During this time, it has total jurisdiction over the body. It can abort the fetus or cause a miscarriage if it feels incompatible, if, for example, some newly created karmic condition by the parents, particularly the mother, alters the original plan. If its karmic plan is just to have the experience through gestation, it can be stillborn.

The Soul, beginning its experiences in this body, usually enters on the baby's first breath. The Soul also determines how far it will enter the physical body. It can hover above the body until it finally enters, knowing that it has to get in by a certain time in order to fulfill the destiny. This, in a way, validates astrology, which deals in time cycles and planetary influences. The only caution about using astrology as a source of information is that you don't use it to avoid the lessons and learnings that are awaiting you. In fact, regardless of astrological information, you still have your karmic lessons. If you don't act in and out of a loving consciousness, astrology won't help you. Only acts of loving will.

The veil of forgetfulness for the basic self falls at around seven to eight years of age. From this point on, the basic self no longer has a complete working memory of the life plan. It is now that the high self carries it. The plan is still with the basic, but at the level of dormant awareness. The conscious self comes in as a total blank. Memory is the domain of the basic self, which slowly feeds the conscious self as it gets trained to handle its responsibilities on the physical level.

It is valuable to think of your basic as somebody who grew to around four years of age and then stopped. In other words, don't let a four-year-old child run your adult body. That would be like letting a four-year-old drive a huge diesel truck down the highway. Overwhelming, to say the least. Very dangerous, to say the most.

The relationship between the basic and conscious selves can be delicate. The basic can run things if the conscious self relinquishes responsibility. For example, the basic self can steal and make the conscious feel guilty. Then the conscious represses this, and this repressed energy becomes a block between the high self and the conscious self. Because the high self is the communicator with Soul, you are then blocking yourself from God. That's perhaps the closest thing I know to sin—blocking communication with God.

The Mystical Traveler Consciousness is aware of this blocked communication and fits into the high, conscious, and basic selves as an energy *without interfering.* It can clear things only if you call on it from the conscious self and high self. Part of this calling is the expression of spiritual exercises. The Traveler also works with you on the spiritual levels through such techniques and services as aura balances, Soul Awareness Discourses and Tapes, seminars, and innerphasings, all of which are designed to loosen and lift that which is stuffed, in order to permit the flow of Spirit.

Spirit lifts and rises. When you rise and come into the spirit of the occasion, you become part of the majesty of God, in which the basic, conscious, and high selves ultimately cooperate in loving harmony.

Destiny or Free Will

Don't think that all your actions and inactions are pre-determined. Only the life plan, within a complex structure, is prepared. On the way are what we call free choices. Free choices *on the way.* On the way to where? On the way to where you started—your spiritual home, your source, your Soul, the heart of God, you.

Have you done this before? Certainly. You have had many opportunities to fulfill your ultimate destiny, and for many different reasons (most often spelled e-g-o) you chose not to go all the way. Now, once again, you are faced with the ultimate choice of completion and eternal joy or, if you choose, reembodiment on this difficult planet. It's your choice.

There is a veil of forgetfulness from one incarnation to the next in order for you to have a better opportunity of fulfilling the choice you made in Spirit. For if you saw everything from above to below, from your past lives to the present, it might be more difficult and more painful than you could handle in your current state of awareness. If you did not forget, you might feel bad about the things you did to other people and yourself in previous lifetimes, and the sadness could weigh you down so much that you would be unable to do anything this lifetime.

Spirit is not interested in guilt or blame. Guilt is a valueless commodity unless you use it as an indicator of information, thus avoiding guilt-producing acts.

Some people think they have free will, or choice, regarding when they will die. Before you embodied, when you met with the high self and the akashic board, it was determined how long you would live and when you would die. (Not *how* you would die. Perhaps that might be free choice. Perhaps.) Even those people who have tried to commit suicide "before their time," that is, before the time agreed upon with the high self, do not die. Instead, they get their stomachs pumped and come to with a terrible hangover, still alive. You cannot die unless the high self is in accord. It doesn't care how you die (e.g., heart attack, car wreck, or in your sleep) because the Soul never dies. It always lives. So there is no caring about the body from the level of the high self because it is recognized that at the present time, it is the body's nature to die.

If people who consider suicide understood the plan, they would not commit suicide; they would realize that you can kill yourself 100 times and that you still have to reembody 101 times. Your ego may resist, but when there is karma to work out, there is no avoidance. It will be worked out.

You notice that the ego has been mentioned numerous times. I am not discounting the value of ego. It permits us to go where "angels fear to tread." It encourages us to take risks. It supports us when we strive for achievement. It also supports and creates recognition for recognition's sake. If we feed our ego with our energy, then, along with our lower self, we truly co-create a monster. We get hooked on the ego's adrenaline, which is recognition, applause, and compliments. Fool's gold. After a while, the addict who is hooked on ego is no longer in a position to recognize whether compliments and affirmation are true or false. After a while, it doesn't matter. Then you may become a total junkie, a slave of the ego.

The ego is a product of mental and emotional interaction. The ego seems to work independently of your mind and Soul. In fact, the ego is the enemy of Soul transcendence. Most people think they are the ego. You can stop the ego, but you cannot stop yourself. You can hold your breath so long that you pass out, and then you will start breathing again. When you pass out, the ego is gone (it is in the mental-emotional process), so that which is making you breathe is who you are.

You are not the ego, which looks for approval. Who you truly are needs no approval. When you just are, there is no validation required because you just are. On the highest level, it is known as I AM. God.

Above the Soul Realm

Starting from the highest of the highs, first there is Spirit. Out of Spirit came God; down from God came many levels.

There are at least 27 levels from God before we get to the Soul realm. These levels have various names and manifestations of God in them. They are not verbal. We call them the nameless realms, the inaccessible realms, the unavailable places; you have to guess at the rest because there is no vocabulary term. Except for the ancient Adamic language, the way you will get to the nature of this is by telepathy and, for a select few who choose back in ways of Spirit, by experience.

Soul Realm

Soul is another way of saying I AM. It is the highest level of consciousness available on the physical level. The Soul is intelligence. It just knows. In Hinduism it is also called Atman, a Sanskrit term meaning your essence, who you are.

The Soul exists on all levels—physical, astral, causal, mental, and etheric. While the Soul is the weakest aspect in the physical world, it is the only one that is on all the levels. So if you're going to live on any level, it makes sense that the best place to live is in Soul.

Soul travel refers to out-of-body experiences that can occur while you are involved in spiritual exercises, while you are sleeping, and, at times, even while you are awake and functioning, doing tasks that involve only basic-self habits. Soul travel is that divine experience where the spiritual essence of you is literally traveling in the inner realms. As you travel to the higher realms, you receive experiences and information that strengthen your spiritual heart and can complete karma. Part of the work that goes on within the Movement of Spiritual Inner Awareness is developing the ability to bring back awareness of our Soul-travel experiences.

Many times, particularly with new initiates, the awareness is limited, but, nonetheless, you still Soul travel often. For instance, have you ever awakened in the morning, and then your first awareness was sitting at your desk at work, wondering how you got there? Your basic self may have handled all the automatic tasks (from dressing to driving) while you were Soul traveling. (I don't encourage Soul travel while driving a car. I'd rather you drive in awareness and Soul travel from a stationary position.)

Once we know and accept the possibility and experience of Soul travel, we realize it is a natural occurrence, and in that recognition, we increase our ability to do this.

We have access to all information. When someone invents something, makes a great discovery, or comes up with an evolutionary theory that affects the world, that person is tapping into the universal knowledge that has always existed. It just took that particular person's getting out of the way (ego, conditioning, gender, economic status, and all other limiting frames of mind) and becoming a channel for the information.

Geniuses are actually those beings with clear channels for this information. From Mozart and Einstein to Shakespeare and Emerson, from e.e. cummings to Lao-tzu and Joan of Arc—each one tapped into a source, otherwise known as the Soul energy. The Soul, which is the omni-intelligence source, knows it all.

Through the Soul, we are all connected. Those beings who are so-called geniuses and those beings who are so-called idiots are totally connected in Spirit. It's just that one has tapped into Soul energy on a particular, different level. Different, not better.

Notice that I said on a particular level. A person may tap into the Soul-level source of art, science, literature, music, and so on. The thing that makes it universal is the essence of God, which, on the physical level, we sometimes call humanity. When we watch a movie or television show, see a painting, or read a book that moves us in our hearts, we are probably being touched by that humanity of Soul energy, of God, that has been channeled through the medium.

When you are in the levels below Soul, primarily you are aware that you *see* the Light, and it is beautiful. When you reach the Soul realm you are *part* of the Light. You are impressed with the Light, which is actually the Sound Current, the audible Sound of God, which exists on all levels and can be seen as various colors.

The connection that ultimately merges within each of us is the primary ingredient of Soul, a neutral, infinite, unconditional loving, in God.

There are approximately 4.5 billion people on this planet, and maybe 40 get established as high as the Soul level. This may change as beings of consciousness and commitment meet in spiritual exercises and service, awakening to the Mystical Traveler in each of them.

When you get to Soul, you can bring into the physical the Soul knowledge of what is, and you can correct the things in life that need correction. You can make your life wonderful and beautiful and joyous. You learn how to manage on all the levels, from Soul on down, moment by moment, decision by decision, knowing that there are consequences coming that will challenge you and that can be handled, experienced, and corrected when need be. It is possible to live your life in Soul consciousness right now, from the physical to the Soul and back again, co-creating health, wealth, and happiness.

Etheric Realm

*In the etheric realm, there are
the astral, causal, mental, etheric,
and Soul levels.*

Descending from the Soul realm, we come to the void that peaks the etheric realm. In this area, we may experience what we call goblins, ghosts, and other things that go bump in the night. This is the area with which psychologists, psychiatrists, and psychoanalysts work. This void and dark is one of the areas into which we repress our negativity.

This void separates the Soul realm, the spiritual world, from the psychic-material worlds. In order to go through the void into the Soul realm and *live there, never having to incarnate again,* you have to prove yourself by dissolving all the karma.

Everything below the Soul level reincarnates. If you get as high as the etheric, you may live there ten thousand years and think you are in heaven. One day, however, you will awaken down on the physical realm as a little baby.

The void between the etheric and Soul is dark, except in the reflective part. The cosmic mirror (the reflection) shows everything below it. Some of the levels mirrored, such as Summerland in the astral world, are so magnificent that they are often traps that keep us from the Soul level. By the time you evolve to the etheric realm, you have gone through the brilliance of the Lords of the astral, causal, and mental realms, and now you are reflected as the brightest thing in sight. The fact is, however, that you are still not in the Soul realm.

Everything that has not been cleared in the physical, astral, causal, and mental levels is projected onto the cosmic mirror. It may appear as dreadful circumstances that evoke drastic feelings and that seem to be reality. This is not reality. It is only a reflection. Although just a reflection, it is not to be ignored or dismissed. This information reveals the illusions people create and their attachments to glamour and to lust, envy, and the other "deadly sins." By using this information, you can balance the action by learning detachment, by letting go and letting God. Before you get to Soul, you will have to clean up all attachments and addictions.

Some settle in the etheric realm, thinking this is heaven as they experience God's presence. God is, indeed, present in the etheric, as It is in all the other realms, but this is not the heaven that we consider eternal life. Eternity exists only in the positive realms, Soul and above. In order to get there, a person must work through all the different levels of the etheric (the unconscious) and the areas that are impossible to define in words. The guidance of the Mystical Traveler Consciousness in this realm is of *primary* value in getting to Soul.

Out of the etheric level come the Siddha powers, the ability to do what we call magic: make objects appear and have disembodied voices speak. Such magic is just such magic, and it comes from a negative realm. Only the Soul realm and above is positive. Regardless of the tricks performed right before your eyes, I suggest that you carefully check out anything you get from any source, in order to determine if the communication and input from that being bring you more than the maya of Spirit.

How can you check that out? Does participation with a teaching bring you more joy and abundance on the inner and outer levels? Does the information received and applied evoke more loving in your life? If not, you may be playing with fire rather than upliftment.

Inside you is the micro; simultaneously, there is the macro out there—worlds without end. Jesus said, "In my Father's house are many mansions."[4] You are sitting as a pivot point between two dynamic areas. Your difficulty arises if one starts to take more control than the other. Your task is to make yourself available to both the macro and the micro. How do you do that? Spiritual exercises, prayer, loving, caring, and serving here in the physical world. You make yourself available by taking the needful first step.

One of the first steps is forgiving. Forgive yourself and the other person. Forgive the emotions you ran on someone else. Forgive the other person. For to err is human; to forgive, divine.

Through such expressions and spiritual exercises, you can transcend the last negative realm, the etheric, and move through the void into the Soul realm.

4. John 14:2, King James Version

Mental Realm

*In the mental realm, there are
the astral, causal, mental, etheric,
and Soul levels.*

*The Lord of the Mental realm is
thousands of times more brilliant
than the Lord of the astral realm.*

The actions of the mental realm involve mentalizing, not necessarily thinking. These mental exercises can be fun, productive in terms of looking at things from different points of view, and often futile, as in mental gymnastics.

The mental realm consciousness can retain everything from sports statistics to a commercial jingle selling a product. This may be positive, particularly if you want to master trivia, but it is not to your highest advantage when it distracts you from spiritual exercises.

For instance, you may call in the Light and chant Ani-Hu,[5] but the mind (otherwise known as monkey mind or blabber mind) can go on forever. In this instance, the expression and commitment of the conscious self are required to focus on the holy names of God.

Most human beings have a degree they don't know has been granted. It's called a D.D.M., a divine degree in management. We are here to manage our bodies, our emotions, and our minds. Most people choose, however, not to manage their emotions. Welcome to the causal creepies. You don't think you get those? Oh no? Have you ever screamed at someone because they weren't doing what you wanted them to do, in the way you wanted them to

5. Ani-Hu is pronounced "ahn-eye you." *Ani* evokes empathy, and *Hu* is an ancient name of God.

do it, and at the time you wanted them to do it? Did you scream at your husband, your wife, your mother, your father, your child? I can hear you: "But they were wrong. They were doing. . . ." Maybe they were. Maybe their behavior did have error in it. From where are you coming? Perfection? Are you perfect? Is anyone on this planet perfect? Of course not.

Maybe we are the divine mistake, here to learn the perfection. The paradox is that perfection is unavailable on this physical level. Only in the positive realms—Soul and above—is perfection available. So you may as well relax, *express yourself toward excellence,* and give yourself and your loved ones room and permission to make mistakes. If you do, you're on the way up. If you don't, you are courting anxiety and depression because you are not choosing to exercise your D.D.M. You are not managing your emotions.

Management is not all that complex. When, in the face of your commitment to lose weight, you have the urge to eat another piece of chocolate cake, manage the urge. Right now, this forkful is the challenge to your management. You don't have to worry about the last meal or tell yourself that tomorrow you will fast. Now is the time for management. You can take managerial control over your body at any given moment. That *is* part of your divine inheritance. For you to claim it takes doing.

There is intellect in the mental realm, but not necessarily intelligence. Intelligence is in the Soul's domain. Intelligence is knowing. In order to do what it takes to manage your life, you have to go to the source of strength. It is not on the outside. It is not subscribing to the latest diet fad. The last one didn't do it for you because you were putting your energy into outside cures. If you take it from the inside, you are then able to create what you really choose. You have within you the ability to create.

The trap often created in this realm is the attitude that "if I think it, it is so." That is nonsense. We can spend a great deal of time intellectualizing about a great many things, and we can still be absolutely in error about what is. Before Columbus, many intellectuals said the world was flat.

We often determine through our intellectual process how someone should behave, dress, talk, and act. This is often based on the mores pertaining to the time and place and the person's gender, age, economic circumstances, and race. We deprive the person and ourselves of the original experience of their beingness. We can reason and justify our intellectual point of view forever. Well, almost forever, for in Spirit there is a time when the intelligence calls forth the being, and all the positions that we have defended for all the lifetimes will crumble in the face of God. I suggest you address that possibility now, rather than wait for that forever.

Numerous beings have seen God on this mental level. Your learning and the conditioning you embraced on the lower levels often determine what you see on this realm. If you were taught that you will experience hell when you die and if you accept that, you may create that purifier. Or, depending upon your training, you may see Buddha; if you're Christian, Jesus; if Jewish, Moses or Joshua or another being; if Hindu, you may see Shiva, Vishnu, or Brahma.

As beautiful and seductive as is this Lord of the mental realm, if you stop here, you will incarnate back to planet Earth for additional lessons.

Causal Realm

In the causal realm, there are
the astral, causal, mental, etheric,
and Soul levels.

The Lord of the causal realm
(often called Jehovah)
is at least a thousand times more
brilliant than the Lord of the
astral realm.

The causes of those things that happen in this physical realm originate in the causal realm, which is the level of cause and effect. The seeds of karma are contained here. People often think that most of our troubles come from this level, but, from a higher perspective, those troubling situations are actually balancing actions. The equivalent Judeo-Christian concept for karma is that "whatever a man sows, that he will also reap."[6]

This is the area of emotions. Everything you have to work out in the world comes out of this level. Everything. Regardless of whether you are higher than this level (in the mental or the etheric), it all comes from the causal.

Although the causal realm is not the highest realm, it is still one of the most important because feelings and emotions run people more often than does their thinking. You feel inclined to do something; then, after you do it, you

6. Galatians 6:7, Revised Standard Version

wonder why you were crazy enough to do that. (People who have psychiatric or psychological difficulties often come with problems out of the astral or causal level.)

The emotive body, which is in the causal area, produces emotional energy that has no intellect. As an analogy, water moves in an energy pattern that has no intellect. Similar to that is the energy of the causal area that we call emotions; the emotional energy carries you along through all areas of this world, and it has no intelligence. These emotions are like a thread that weaves throughout the entire fabric of your life. On this golden thread resides your DNA and RNA programming of inherited predisposition toward those areas (karmic situations) that you are here to balance in this lifetime (or in 24,365 additional ones, if you so choose).

Are Feelings Valid?

On this causal level, we create disturbances that are reflected into the physical level, the barometer being our feelings. How many times have you defended yourself with "I just felt that way. I couldn't help it."? The fact is, we *can* help it, but usually we don't; usually we give total dominion to the causal energies and let them run our lives.

Because of our feelings and emotions, we let interpretation run us. We can say good morning to someone, and if they just grunt and don't return our smile, we react emotionally. We let our emotions run rampant and think, "That stuck up man. I said hello, I smiled, I was ready to share the good news of the day, and he just grunts as if I'm not alive. I'll show him who's not alive!" Then we treat him as if he were better off dead—all because of our interpretive supposition based on the expectations of our emotions and what our feelings told us.

Rather than withhold, you could simply ask the man, "Is there anything wrong this morning? Is there something I can do to ease what might be troubling you?" You might discover that he was up most of the night taking care of his wife who was ill, and the lack of sleep and his concern for his wife caused him to appear rude.

If you ever have a similar experience, it might assist everyone if you just communicated rather than growled. You could say, "Excuse me. I had a rough time last night and I'm worrried about a loved one." You could then see how you might be supported in tenderness. The sad fact is, however, that many people would rather withhold than take the time and effort—in awareness—to bypass those famous feelings.

Each organization (and large family group) has in it at least one person who will attempt to sabotage the organization by withholding pertinent information until a crucial time. This is called management by crisis. The information is sometimes shared too late to be used, and then it's called management by default. When that starts to take place, it is time to isolate the individual and let them know—if it's a business—that they will be fired before the business collapses.

In a family, if a child is creating dissension between the parents, for example, the mother and father have the choice either to give in to emotions and feelings and to bicker and blame each other ("It's your kid") or to bypass the emotions and to sit down and talk. They can be straight with the child: "You are not going to continue to cause dissension in this house. Before we get divorced you will have to change your act or leave."

If the child is not old enough, let them know there are homes that take in minors. A tough stance? Sure, but the conditions that you create, promote, or allow through indulging the causal creepies and by working from your emotions often create tough situations. Your choice is to be a victim, by being stuck in a particular lower realm, or to use the situation as information and transcend the limitations of the realm, inside and outside: on Earth as in heaven.

Withholds Hold You Back

If you withhold yourself from your life, you are withholding the support of Spirit. By placing your energy into the limitations of the physical, you are disregarding the spiritual area where the keys to success are found. If you ignore that area, you must pay the price. It may be called tuberculosis, bad back, dis-ease. Spirit doesn't care because there are no emotional levels in Spirit. Since there are emotional levels in you, why not use them to your advantage and emotionally choose to live a happy, healthy, and wealthy life? In other words, I do suggest you care.

If you don't withhold your awareness, integrity, and loving from yourself, you'll be surprised how easily life can be handled. The body itself is inherently capable of maintaining and healing itself. That mechanism is inbuilt. God made us out of prime stuff. There's nothing second-hand in our physical makeup, although we have a built-in obsolescence, called either death or passage to the higher realms of Spirit.

No matter how spiritual you claim to be, you can still go crazy with emotions if you don't strengthen the spiritual inner connection and exercise the conscious self's will-power. Most people give in to the basic self's won't-power and erupt in emotional energy that only vents anger, hurt, and dismay. What they are left with after this expression is anger, hurt, and dismay, as well as a lonely, exhausted feeling of energy depletion.

It is your choice. If you wish to rely on the emotional energy and ride it like a flood or, in some cases, Niagara Falls, you can go with that energy. I suggest caution. Evoke intelligence to determine if you really want to go along with your emotions or if you want to just stand next to the observation railing of your conscious self, hold tight, and observe the emotions flooding by, without your participation. Is that difficult? In the beginning, yes. In time, it gets easier. How? Practice.

Astral Realm

*In the astral realm, there is
an astral, causal, mental, etheric,
and Soul level. In the causal level,
of the astral, there could be
ten million levels.*

*The Lord of the astral level is
more brilliant than 16 of the suns
in the sky.*

*St. Peter, "the gatekeeper," is
in the astral realm.*

The astral realm is the area where the imagination and concomitant feelings reside. There is no physical in the astral world, although the astral body does resemble this physical body. It is not in the condensed energy form of the physical body, however.

The astral body has a double body around it that has all our unconscious baggage of this world. Part of that package is everything that we have done and not done which is hanging around us. Excess weight is sometimes a direct result of undone things. We have tucked them into the baggage around us. As soon as we handle something, we often feel as if a load lifted off our back. We are also in a position to lose weight physically and to lighten up emotionally, as well.

That unconscious body is identified with the physical body, getting its energy off the astral field. When the physical body dies, that unconscious body wraps itself around the astral body. If the astral body doesn't have enough power to shake it loose, what is called an earthbound spirit is often produced. It can hang around for a thousand years.

Part of what I teach, Soul transcendence, is an inner knowing of how to leave the body when we travel to the higher realms. We know how to use our willpower and shake those unconscious energies loose. We can then drop the astral body and evolve to the causal body. As we continue transcending, we relieve ourselves of our causal body and come to the mental body, etc. And in this case, *etc* stands for eternal traveling consciousness.

When the Mystical Traveler comes to you in Spirit on the astral level, it comes in the semblance of my physical body. That form is radiant because it has the Soul energy with it. You can see it when you close your eyes because when you close your eyes you go to the astral world. You may wonder if it's your imagination or if it's real. On the astral level, it is real. On this physical level, it is imagination.

You cannot have physical experiences in the astral world, although if we were in the astral world right now and I offered you a glass of vintage wine, it might taste better on that level because the senses are sharper. In a way, you might qualify as a better wino in the astral world than in the physical, if that is your choice. If you're going to be a drunkard, perhaps the astral world is the best place. At least you can't fall down physically. In the astral, it's more like floating.

Insomnia comes from the mental level in the astral realm. The astral mind continually mentalizes about issues; combining with imagination, it affects the body and, at times, the adrenal glands, causing the nervous system to react. If the pituitary gland has been involved in too much mentalizing, there is a stream of action from the mind with no apparent way to control it. One way to handle this situation is to actually get out of bed and do strenuous physical exercises. This will use the excess adrenaline in the body. Then it is possible to lie down and rest.

Most psychics function from this astral level, which is a level of phenomena, levitation, and table-raising. Because this is the realm of imagination, which has a powerful influence on the physical realm, these kinds of phenomena feed off the imagination.

Most dreams occur in the astral level. Another way we imagine, or image-in, is by daydreaming. When we close our eyes, we go immediately into the astral level. It takes place automatically. Daydreams actually weave in and out of the astral, causal, and physical worlds.

Daydreaming is one of the most profound experiences we can have when we choose that method of getting away from unpleasant things. Children use this tool often. My attitude is not to criticize or judge them for doing that. Daydreaming is not wasting time. It can be quite useful in giving the person time to manage their emotions through getting away from a source of emotional difficulty.

Daydreaming also permits the creative elements to fuse and produce more easily without the conscious self, ego, and judgment in the way. Part of the creative process involves getting those aspects (conscious self, ego, and judgment) out of the way so that the creative forces can flow freely. The structuring comes in later when you translate the vision into a scientific theory, onto canvas, or into a book. Einstein daydreamed, as did Edison and many other creative, inventive people. Adults don't feel comfortable calling it daydreaming, however, so we invented another, more mature word to rationalize the act. We call it preoccupation.

Another expression describing the creative act is channeling, for that is actually what we are doing. We have let ourselves move past conditioning and have permitted the energy of Soul to come through the etheric, mental, causal, and astral levels into an experience/vision/concept that just is. When we have channeled the energy of Soul in this way, we can feel euphoric because we are totally present on all the levels in a *now* experience, channeling an artistic or scientific vision with the underlying essence of spiritual truth.

There are similar moments when a loving couple engages in sexual intercourse. At those rare times, when the egos and expectations are bypassed and only the loving is given and received, orgasm can be that moment when all levels of consciousness are together, at one point.

This is not usually the case because sexual intercourse is often based on lust, not on loving, and techniques for sexual fulfillment are used more often than are expressions of loving care. More often than not, the person participating in the sexual act will be distracted and, while continuing the physical expression, may be residing in the mental, causal, or astral level. How do you become capable of bypassing the conditioning, the demands, and the expectations? Not by forcing yourself or pretending. It is a process of awareness, acceptance, and action.

The top part of the astral realm, called Summerland, is what most Christian religions and other orthodox religions call heaven. You may live here 1,500 years and have to turn away from the Lord of the astral level because the reflection would be so bright—and that is still in the psychic-material worlds. Even though you might think you are in heaven eternally, you will generally incarnate back to the physical level as an infant.

Physical Realm

The first level, from your present viewpoint, is the physical, material level. It's called you. But it's not who you are. For that information, you have to check out the Soul level. For now, however, the physical is where you are. Touch this book. This is physical. The physical is also condensed spiritual energy. Being more material than spiritual, however, it has the vibration of change. It will not hold as it is. It is designed to change, to age, to decay, to die, to be just an energy blip in the universe.

The physical is not in the astral, causal, mental, etheric, or Soul realm, but in the physical we have all the others, *which is why we are here.* It is only on this realm that we have it all together, enabling us to jump into Spirit from one place. Of course, the doing is more difficult than the saying. It is difficult from here because the springboard is the physical body, propelling us into that which is not physical.

The physical level doesn't even run itself. The physical level is run by the astral, for it is the astral to which we first have to ascend on our journey home. From the physical, we cannot control other levels on the divine learning mission. From this physical realm, however, we can learn what we have to, as we transcend into Spirit.

We choose to incarnate here precisely because we can have all the experiences in this level, whereas we cannot have the physical experiences in the astral, causal, mental, etheric, or Soul level.

Experience is the master teacher.

The Mystical Traveler Consciousness

*In creation
God was just one,
in one location
called the Spirit.*

God wanted to know Itself on all levels of creation. Through eons of time, It created levels below It and extended Itself into those levels. As It extended Itself into the levels, It also had to maintain the levels spiritually, and so the Mystical Traveler Consciousness has always been a spiritual guide on every level above the physical. The Traveler works with the Soul in awakening it to its divine destiny.

Every Soul comes out of God. Each of us has the essence of God within. That is the Soul, an essence of God. There are people who think the Soul is in trouble because they see all the negative levels below Soul. The Soul is not in trouble. Being an essence of God, the Soul cannot destroy itself because God will not destroy Itself. And, in time, each human being will realize that they are, indeed, the Soul, not the lower levels of consciousness.

For example, a person who lives in Brooklyn may think of herself as a Brooklynite, and then, when she gets more objective, she will think of herself as a New Yorker. Raising her sights higher, she might identify herself as an American and just keep going: a North American, a Western

Hemispherean, a citizen of the world, a member of the universe, a child of God.

You see, no matter what lower levels we identify as being us, whether we attach our egos to our race, our gender, our nationality, our bank account, our profession, our avocation, our physical or mental abilities, when we come right down to it (or actually, right up to it) we are all the same thing—*a child of God*—and our true home is in the Soul realm. All those levels below are just our individual learning levels, designed to assist us in returning to where we started, the source, the I Am that I Am.

On the level of God comes what is known as the Mystical Traveler Consciousness. At present, that is the consciousness I carry. The Traveler is aware on all levels simultaneously. It has authority and power over everything on every level down to the physical. On the physical level, it does not. Many of the Mystical Travelers, when they get to the physical level, get crucified or assassinated. (I am not a candidate for that; I am just giving you spiritual history.)

This I AM is another term used synonymously for the Mystical Traveler and the Soul. It is in every body, but not everybody is aware of that. In each of these lower levels, there is a Lord or God. Christ came as one. There is also a Christ on every level. There is a Christ down here on the physical level. His physical name was Jesus, but that was not his real name. His real spiritual name might be the I Am of the I Am.

Working with the Mystical Traveler Consciousness as a guide is of primary importance in transcending the etheric realm, through the void, into Soul. To get through the etheric void into the Soul realm, you must be able to go through the Rukmini canal. The Mystical Traveler Consciousness, which simultaneously works on all levels above the physical, will be your strengthener as St. Peter checks your karmic records, particularly if you are an initiate of the Traveler.

Initiates of the Traveler are given the name of the Lord in each realm as they are initiated into that level, and when the initiate chants that name, the vibration of that Lord presents It of Itself. The initiate then rides on that energy through that level under the protection of that Lord, *who is actually the Mystical Traveler on that realm.*

When you see or hear the Traveler for the first time (in the physical form or, quite often, in the dream state, on tape or television, or from a person telling you about it), you usually get your astral initiation. At this time, you have the choice of consciously working with the Traveler to clear karma this lifetime and transcend to Soul, or passing on the opportunity. If you do not make the choice this lifetime, you will have many other opportunities in future embodiments. As long as there is a physical planet, there shall always be a Mystical Traveler Consciousness to guide those who choose to do what it takes to get to Soul.

When most of the karma is worked out on the astral level, you get initiated to the next level (see the section on Initiation), and you are given additional names of the Lord to chant. There is a total of five names. When you get the fifth name, that is the Soul realm.

The Mystical Traveler hears your chanting and, as the Lord of the realm of your present spiritual awareness (and above), the Traveler gives energy down to you in response. He goes under many names—Jehovah, Jesus Christ, Allah, Rama, Krishna—depending upon the conditioning and vocabulary of your particular culture or country. A tribe of American Indians might call him Monatu. Same being, same God. There are at least 108 names for the Lord.

The Traveler Consciousness has a body on every level, in every universe, on every planet. Even before this earth existed, there were other planets in its place, and the Traveler was present. There are other Souls that exist in other solar systems, in other galaxies, who can travel into this universe as well. The Traveler is also there for them.

In this time period, on a planet called Earth, the Mystical Traveler formed the Movement of Spiritual Inner Awareness (MSIA) as part of its method of reaching people in Spirit on the physical and working with those who choose, assisting them in transcending to the Soul realm.

There are some who can be in MSIA and just get information; in other words, not work with the Traveler on the spiritual levels of ascension. They will gather intellectual data to satisfy themselves on that level, which is still in the negative realms. That's fine with me. Only, if the truth were known (and it is), there is no essence-satisfaction on levels below Soul. On this physical level, consistent satisfaction is not available.

On the Soul level, satisfaction is not a concern because there is nothing negative to use for comparison. The natural, eternal state in Soul is an active comfort of being.

The Traveler offers a technique of connecting into Soul and bringing that awareness right down here to the physical level. It's spiritual exercises, otherwise known as s.e.'s. Those who are interested in transcending these lower levels in actions of commitment and manifestation work with the Traveler through the process of s.e.'s, chanting their initiatory tones and being of service to others.

The Traveler's energy is the essence of Spirit. It is non-inflictive, and it will not enter where it is not invited. In your growing awareness you can awaken to the Mystical Traveler Consciousness, not as an external force, but as that which already exists within you. The Traveler's energy is directed toward your gaining the awareness of that which is your divine heritage.

In contrast to the laws of the physical plane, in Spirit, the more you use the Traveler's guidance, the more you get. The more you awaken to the Traveler within you, the greater are the levels of transcendence. On this physical level, the Traveler's energy comes in the form of unconditional loving; the more you give, the more you get.

The reason I suggest you avail yourself of the Traveler's guidance is simply because I love you. In my love for you, I want that which is for your highest good. By participating with the Traveler, you can lose only that which is negative and temporary and gain only that which is positive and eternal. Those beings who transcend these levels into God's realm, living in Soul eternally, are indeed blessed with that which is for the highest good.

Spiritual Exercises

Spiritual exercises, the technique that permits the Traveler to work with you, is an active process that strengthens the Soul on each level of ascension, bringing awakening to the Soul in an active, dynamic, loving energy. When you participate in the upward spiral of spiritual exercises, you are in high gear by the time you hit the Soul level, and you can't fall back again unless you choose to, which would be by eliminating the expression that got you there: s.e.'s and service expressed in a vibratory frequency of unconditional loving.

In other forms of spiritual pursuit, meditation is a major technique. This is a process that requires a certain physical posture and an effort to be quiet. It is most difficult to be quiet when one has a mind. To still the mind may be the goal of meditation, and when and if this is accomplished, the meditator goes as high as the *etheric* level. When you knock on the door of the Soul level, however, there is much action, not quiet, because the Soul is active. You cannot go through the door, or the Rukmini canal, by passive quietude. You cannot reach the Soul realm in the meditative process.

Don't misunderstand my comments as being negative toward meditation. I find that technique valuable for blood pressure and for relaxation on the physical level. Through meditation, a person can also evolve all the way up to the etheric level. That has a distinct value. Even from the etheric, however, a Soul must reembody to planet Earth. Only when reaching the Soul realm are you in the first positive realm, otherwise known as your true home. Meditation is not designed for that. Spiritual exercises are designed with the specific intention of getting you off the planet for good. And it is good.

As you chant your tones (the ancient names of God), you clear enough karma to evolve to each succeeding level. It is not by your mental, physical, or creative ability that you do this. It is specifically by your putting in the time, loving, and disciplined focus that you do it.

Pure spiritual exercises need be done only 15 minutes a day, but few mortals are capable of pure s.e.'s. By pure, I mean total concentration in total loving devotion. Most disciples of Spirit require two hours a day just to get those 15 minutes. I recommend that those two hours be done in a row in order for you to build up energy and eventually bypass the constant mind chatter.

For a novice, doing two hours of s.e.'s can be difficult. I suggest you don't set yourself up for failure. If you're just starting to do s.e.'s, perhaps you might initially do 40 minutes. Then, in time, work up to 60 minutes. For two or three months, keep extending the time until you have trained yourself to sit in spiritual exercises for two hours. Difficult? Yes. Worth it? Only if you're interested in an eternal existence of joy.

The mind is a marvelous mechanism as long as you enjoy mentalizing and are willing to be limited to this physical plane. When you recognize that there is more than the limitations of the physical plane, you do what it takes to bypass the mind. The mind, smart as it is, will do everything to distract you from bypassing it because it knows that you will leave it behind. For the mind cannot get into Soul.

It's a great game. Great, if you see the paradox and humor and if you love your mind as you say, "Bye-bye. I'm doing my tone. See you later." It's not so great when you give in to your mind and say, "Bye-bye, Soul realm. I'm going to stick down here in the land of mental and physical illusions." Again, as in everything with the Traveler, it's your choice. It's not a matter of brain-washing. It's more a matter of brain-*watching*.

Chanting your initiatory tone or Ani-Hu (empathy/ God) opens you to the loving that you are, regardless of what is happening or not happening in your physical world. I suggest that you chant for about 20 minutes and then listen for about 20 minutes. Sometimes the listening will just be hearing mind chatter, and sometimes you will hear or see other things—words, sentences, images, and sounds.

Do not be dismayed if nothing happens. The simple act of sitting down and doing s.e.'s is a worthy happening in and of itself. In time you will be more aware of Spirit's feedback. Until you reach that fine attunement, know that just the act of doing s.e.'s is perfect. In fact, that is the most important event in your commitment to giving yourself the gift of God.

The Sound
Current

There is a Sound of God on each level, otherwise known as the Sound Current. The Sound is a very high form of ultimate reality. Once you get into the Soul realm and above, the Light is not seen in exactly the same way as it is in the lower realms. It is impressed on you and heard. It is primarily Sound and secondly Light.

Accordingly, on every level of Light, in every plane, in every dimension, there is a keeper of the Sound Current. Appointed by Sat Nam, this is the one who is granted the keys to the Sound Current and who is known as the Mystical Traveler Consciousness. The Traveler has the keys on every realm for the flow of Light and the Sound Current.

You can work with the Light, an essence of Spirit, by calling it in, and if you have been practicing (doing s.e.'s and serving), it will come in to work with you.

The Sound Current does not necessarily work by your calling on it. With the Sound Current, *you* have to move *your* consciousness to it. This doesn't happen by desire. You cannot wish it so or even imagine it into reality. In fact, there is no imagination involved in this process.

There are different sounds that accompany the different levels. Just because you read that the sound on the Soul level is similar to a haunting flute, this doesn't mean that you will hear it. You may mock it up with your imagination, and that's what it will be—an imaginative mock-up. Hearing the Sound Current is hearing the Sound Current, and it is not an act of creative imagination. The Sound Current is an audible form of reality on the inner planes. The part inside you that does the spiritual exercises from a spiritual base cannot be deceived or manipulated. You will hear the sounds when you hear them. The information is simply offered so that you can validate the experience when it happens.

Don't push or judge the quality of your s.e.'s on the basis of whether you hear the sounds, see colors, or have any other experience. You are doing s.e.'s correctly when you do them. The quality improves in relation to your disciplined consistency over a period of time (maybe months, years, decades) and in relation to the quality of loving you express while chanting your tone. There is really no wrong way to do s.e.'s except not to do them.

When you have practiced s.e.'s enough so that you do, indeed, Soul travel, reentry into this physical plane of existence is sometimes difficult. (When your consciousness comes back from s.e.'s and Soul traveling, you may hear a loud popping sound. It might sound like knocking or the slamming of a door.) When you open your eyes and physical sights flood in, accompanied by physical level concerns, you might find this level gross and unattractive. Just remind yourself that you are here on this physical level to solve problems in a loving consciousness.

In time, you can integrate the spiritual and physical worlds. The experiences you have on the spiritual levels, from the colors to the sounds, can be used as a strengthening frame of reference while dealing on the physical level. A guideline that works for both levels is acceptance. Accept what is going on in the physical without judgment and you will be able to handle things much more successfully than ever before. Similarly in Spirit, accept what occurs and what doesn't, with no judgment, and that acceptance will contribute to your spiritual progress.

There are times you might have a craving for information about Spirit, from the mental frame of reference. I will share that information, but know it is just that—information. The mental level is not Soul. When you experience this information, it then becomes your next step to the realm above. I'll share the details of the sounds and colors on the different levels, here as well as in the Chart of the Realms at the back of the book. It is something you need *not* memorize. Just participate in the process of s.e.'s and service, and take the time during spiritual exercises to chant and then listen. In time, you will hear and see what is to be—not necessarily in your desire-pattern time, but in Spirit's time, which is always perfect.

On the astral level, the Sound Current is akin to the whoosh of ocean surf.

On the causal, it's chimes or tinkling bells, a very delicate sound.

In the mental level, it's like running water or a tumbling brook.

In the etheric, it's a buzzing sound, such as made by a bee or a fly.

In the Soul, there is a flutelike sound, but it is not an ordinary flute. It is a haunting, almost drawing-to-you sound. It's not tugging because you'll have no resistance. You *will* go to it. That is the sound referred to in the Bible: "In the beginning was the Word, and the Word was with God, and the Word was God."[7] That is a sound from the Soul level of God, which exists perennially in each person. To hear only takes awakening to that which comes through the Soul.

There are at least 27 levels above Soul with concomitant sounds. When you get above the first level, the sound is like a cool summer wind blowing through easily swaying trees.

7. John 1:1, Revised Standard Version

Above that level, it sounds as if thousands of violins are playing or angels are singing. It is the beautiful sound that is often described in Greek mythology. The allegories of the Sound of God and the sound that comes from the heavens exist in literature throughout recorded time. When Jesus said that the wind comes where it comes and goes where it goes and that no one knows where it comes and where it goes, he was referring to the Sound of God.[8]

When you get above the third level of Soul, into the inaccessible levels, you hear the sound of HU. Just the HU sound. There are also sounds above that, but none can be described in words or reproduced with the HU-man voice. They are inner sounds beyond description on the physical level.

8. John 3:8

Spiritual Liberation

You can have an appetite to experience the Sound Current on these levels, and that may induce you to do what it takes to get here. You are responsible for yourself, your actions, and your individual progression. No one else can do it for you. You can be assisted with strength and guidance from the Mystical Traveler, but neither the Traveler nor any other great teacher can do it for you. At some spiritual point, it is you who must step forward into the Spirit of your true self. Yes, even on this physical level, you are capable of liberation, of freedom in Spirit.

Words won't make you free. Yours, mine, or the words of all the sages, rishis, gurus, saints, and martyrs will not free you. Even physical actions will not make you free, although they will clarify the way of freedom. What makes you free is your experiencing and claiming your own freedom. As you express yourself freely, you create freedom. Freedom is a beingness, a state of existence. Freedom is here, right now.

If you are reading this and are distracted from the experience you get while reading this, you need practice. Practice the action of focus. Place your intellect, your emotions, your body—your entire self—here and now. When you are in the only place that Spirit exists, which is here and now, you are then available to your freedom. If you wait for the dispensation of Spirit, or your divorce, or when you move, or when your kids grow up and leave home, or when you lose weight, or when you get a raise, or whenever, you may have to wait until whenever, which may be four incarnations from now.

Spiritual liberation is available here, right now. Use your own consciousness and, if you need assistance, work with the consciousness of the Mystical Traveler. The Traveler cannot violate your consciousness. It will give you the keys as rapidly as you open to receive them. Some, in their lust for spiritual progression, may lay claim to being ready. I can understand and empathize with this. I also know that Spirit knows, regardless of your earnest desires or ego.

If you come to the Traveler on a level of deceit or ego, the deceit or ego is returned to you. You will get your fill of ego and deception until you recognize the process and stop creating it. The Mystical Traveler Consciousness reflects exactly what you put out. If you ask for the truth, then demonstrate the truth. If you ask for the truth and demonstrate a lie, your actions will speak louder than words, and the lie will be laid at your doorstep.

Those who had the keys of Light and Sound in biblical times are the master forces of freedom working with the Traveler right now. All the forces of Spirit are working with you for one intended purpose: that you totally awaken to that which already is—the Light and Sound of God, which is within you at this very moment.

If you can get this, you might understand that what you consider to be problems that distract you from being present in your own joy are actually situations that can be changed whenever you are ready to do what it takes to experience the presence of Spirit. When that occurs, you will be in a position to experience the Sound Current.

As you connect to the Sound Current, you are more open to receive the inner teachings. The inner teachings clarify and strengthen you in Spirit, and then you connect to the Sound Current on even higher levels.

Some people have difficulty with this because they give credence to the mind, which doesn't comprehend this experience. This experience is incomprehensible from the mental viewpoint. I'm talking about the Soul realm, far above the negative levels of the mental realm. If the mind tells you that what you are experiencing (the Sound Current) is just an illusion, I suggest you shrug off your mind by saying, "So what. Call it what you will." For if it *is* the Sound Current, call it illusion or abracadabra, regardless of a name, the experience is a level of joy and essence that is home, whose address is in the Soul realm and whose land-Lord is God.

You will want to work this spiritual process past the mind's resistance. As you discipline yourself in trust, the mind will eventually have no choice but to step aside and let the higher forces rule. To receive the Sound Current, put yourself in a position to receive it. Recognize and accept that you are a child of God and are worthy of being at one with the loving, highest forces in existence. In that recognition, commit to the discipline; literally sit down and *do* spiritual exercises as a habit that the conscious self creates, the basic self respects, and the high self supports.

Do this and you have only You to gain.

Colors of the Realms

When the Sound of God comes down and manifests, it may create a color, which might appear like a flame. On the astral level, the flame could have pink and gold in it. That is what happened at the time of the Pentecost, when the winds of heaven came down and the colors manifested above the disciples. That was the Holy Spirit manifesting through the magnetic Light. (See the Chart of the Realms at the end of the book.)

The color of the physical realm is green.

In the astral, it is pink or rose.

On the causal, it is orange or pale salmon.

In the mental, it is blue.

In the etheric, it is a violet purple.

In the Soul level, there is a gradation of color: gold, light gold, pale gold, and clear.

The Mystical Traveler, who originates above Soul, comes in on purple so that it can be seen, and it also transmutes to the next level below and above, simultaneously.

Chanting Your Tone

The best time to chant may be between 3:00 and 5:00 a.m., and I know many who make beautiful spiritual progress who chant between 6:00 and 8:00 each morning. The issue of prime importance is, however, that you do chant the sacred names of God each day, for a consistent period of time. As you chant, you gain more in the spiritual world, which is commutable, meaning that it becomes available to use as part of your physical expression.

Sometimes you will have an experience of moving into Soul and back to this level and not have a memory of it. You only know/feel/intuit that something, indeed, occurred. In the Movement of Spiritual Inner Awareness we work on expanding our awareness to Soul and back again, so that when we return to this level, we are conscious of our spiritual experiences.

Doing this is not a matter of using the standard memory-pattern energy. It is a new yet ancient technique in which the Soul extends itself as a vortex of energy, on and on, more and more, until you have learned how to stay in Soul and all the other levels simultaneously. You can be totally present, here and now, and simultaneously be in the physical and in Soul.

Just as the Traveler resides in all levels, so is there a Christ Consciousness on each level. It is each person's divine destiny to share that consciousness in awareness. Actually, you already do. My work, as the Mystical Traveler, is just to awaken you to that which already is.

There is only one way I know of that ensures your co-creation of this ongoing awakening: spiritual exercises.

Regardless of your affluence, no matter how much money you can spend for regenerative shots in Switzerland or Mexico, the body will still corrupt and decay. In the spiritual world, the least thing you do will outlast anything in the material world. Spirit cannot be destroyed. Regardless of any and every effort, the body will die according to the karmic law.

If you are working with the Mystical Traveler, it will work with you to complete all your karma this lifetime, enabling you to complete your destiny and return to the heart of God for eternity. This *is* work. It is not a matter of getting clearance two minutes before you die. You must create the space for the Traveler to work with you. This is done by serving, expressing unconditional love, and chanting your tone.

Spiritual Hierarchy

When the body, mind, and spirit are in harmony, you have reached a spiritual attunement in your beingness. You don't have to guess if and when that occurs for you. There is no guessing. You will know by the experience. When you experience Spirit's presence within you, there is always a side effect. It's called joy. When you are in harmony, you will experience joy along with its companion, a sense of peace.

This is not the static peace of nothingness; rather, it is the kind of quiet that exists within the universal flow. It is not the peace where there is no learning. That isn't peace; that's death. Within the peace of Spirit there is also sandpapering. There is always a perfecting process.

When you are in spiritual harmony, you are the one that is. You are a distinct part of the cosmic flow of this universal intelligence. You are in cooperation with the spiritual hierarchy of the planet.

The following information about the spiritual hierarchy is somewhat technical. It is not offered for rote memorization because the test that comes will not ask questions of detail but will offer experiences for your learning. I caution you not to use the verbal knowledge of this information as spiritual validation of your progress or high spiritual status. The true validation comes in experiential joy, not mental data. Then why share the details? Because there is some part of you that likes esoteric information, and if I can satisfy that and perhaps open your heart a little more on the way, then the sharing is worth it.

Around you are invisible energies known as electrical bodies. Envision these as five circles around your physical body. The five deal with different parts of who you are.

One deals with such things as your last reincarnation. (Actually, you only incarnate once. After that it is reembody.) In fact, your last reincarnation might have been 400,000 years ago.

Another energy form deals with your current history—who you are since that first physical breath, since that moment when the Spirit came into you and you became conscious and alive on this physical plane.

There is another circle of energy that deals with the creative part of you, from artistic to philosophic growth.

Another is concerned with your spiritual advancement.

Then there's the master circle of energy, sort of the executive in charge of all of them.

This group of five, your assigned quintet or band, is your court of influence, serving as commutators. If the cosmic rays coming into this universe didn't go through these commutators, your body would burn. They step down the energy to you according to what you're to do this lifetime. These five are totally aware and are in cooperation with your mission during this lifetime.

Above the band are teachers, or guardian angels. In past lifetimes, many people have been part of a guardian angel group. The interesting thing is that on some level you do recall this active belonging. When you walk down the street or ride a bus or go into a supermarket, you might see someone whom you swear you've never seen before but toward whom you feel a great affinity. A rush comes over you, a feeling of almost loving attraction, of knowing that person on a profound level, even though you've never seen them before. They could have been part of your guardian angel group in a previous lifetime. If you go over and tell them that, they may call a cop and have you arrested. I suggest you just let your heart recognize this and, in joy, enjoy the moment.

While doing spiritual exercises or meditation, you often make direct contact with your band. If you focus on one particular vision, influenced by your culture or religious upbringing, you may get a picture of Buddha, Jesus, or Lord Maitreya. Those are your projections, which is fine because each represents the holy work of Spirit. As one of the Travelers wrote, "A rose by any other name would smell as sweet."

There is usually one teacher to approximately 125,000 bands. In other words, since each person has a band of five, so many people may share the same teacher in Spirit. It's not the band's concern who the teacher is, nor is it yours.

Teachers of Spirit are often regarded and described in superlatives. It is fine to love your teacher in spiritual awareness. From the spiritual heart, devotion to a teacher may be a positive, uplifting action for you. If the loving expressed is one of emotionality, however, there can be a trap within that. If you so emotionally adore and love your teacher, what happens when the teacher dies? You may be stuck in the causal realm with all your emotions. Spirit's way is to emphasize the teachings, not the teacher.

I suggest that the most effective way you can demonstrate love and devotion for your teacher is to exemplify the teachings.

Harmonic Frequency of Spirit

When you enter into an event that is stationary in time and you come into the frequency of it, you have control over it. When you come into an event that is flowing in time and you do not enter into its harmonic frequency, it controls you. Then you may experience the helpless feeling that you sometimes call depression or anger. This is most often demonstrated in relationships with others. Because you don't enter into the harmonic frequency, you are run by your lack of balance, and then you resent the situation and feel depressed, angry, and hurt.

The first law of Spirit is acceptance because it is in the act of acceptance that we come to the harmonic balance. When we judge someone or something, we are rejecting the harmonic frequency of that being or event, and, in the rejection, we are out of balance. When you enter into a frequency of time and events that does not correspond with that of someone else, and when you throw yours against theirs, you are in disharmony or discord, called wars, fighting, invectives, and divorce.

If you can allow the freedom inside you to flow with the cosmic energy, not necessarily as you might like it, but *as it comes through the other person,* you automatically spiritualize yourself. This is the spiritual scientific explanation for acceptance and unconditional loving. The scientific formula might be **A + UL = H 2 + W.** (Acceptance plus Unconditional Loving equal Health, Happiness, and Wealth.)

Of course the thing to do with any theory, as scientists well know, is to create a series of tests to see if it is valid. The tests consist of applying the theory in different circumstances in order to determine the validity of the formula.

I suggest that you be the spiritual scientist and apply the theory of acceptance and unconditional loving. In order to make this a true test, you must take risks. Don't play it so safe that you apply it only to your child, your dog, or other adoring creatures who are reasonably safe and won't challenge the theory. Apply this test to your mate when you are about to enter into an ego disagreement of the "You said," "I said" routine. Apply it to your boss or colleague at work, particularly when there is a different point of view being expressed. Consciously be the scientist. Make the world your lab and make every being in it your guinea pig and see how the theory that $A + UL = H2 + W$ holds up.

The danger in this test is not that the theory isn't up to par, but that the tester may not be up to it. Then you might blame the theory for the failure, when all along it was you who chose not to apply $A + UL$. Then you curse the fates because you are not reaping $H2 + W$. You won't be an exception, if that makes you any more comfortable. I offer that because it is said that misery loves company.

School of Rejection

People seem to have been taught to choose rejection. That is the amazing nature of this earth's school, and too many of us have been docile students. Of course, we can also choose not to choose rejection, but that takes a little more individuality. When we do choose to bypass rejection and go for $A + UL$, we are accessing the positive band around us.

Know, however, that there is a negative correlate. That invisible band could be negative, depending upon where you choose to put your energy. In a later section, you will read about the Lord of this physical realm, Kal Niranjan. This Lord of negativity also loves to play in the astral realm, where this hierarchy resides. Even in relation to the band of energy around you, the nature of the influence, whether positive or negative, the harmonics attuned to—are all your choice.

On this planet, the land of Kal, the negative choice is taught, encouraged, and subliminally programmed. Rejection, hate, anger, lust, and avarice are often the subtext to people's existence, such as it is, time after time. (That's lifetime after lifetime.)

You can make another choice, if you have the courage—and, as I've said, it takes great courage to see the face of God. Choosing acceptance and unconditional loving evokes that harmonic balance that makes the choice well worth it. You won't know until you've tried. Then, when you have tasted of the joy and peace of Spirit, you'll know there is no other way.

Nine Aspects of Planet Earth

The spiritual, mental, and physical levels are sub demands under the auspices of a prime demand. The prime demand is to unite all levels in you as the spiritual form. None of this, as yet, involves Soul because the hierarchy I have been describing is primarily in the astral plane. If you go a little higher, into the causal realm, you learn of the nine positive aspects of this planet, which reside in you and only awaken as a result of your activating them. They are love, life, light, peace, power, beauty, joy, harmony, and abundance.

Your spiritual progression may already have different elements of these aspects. If the karmic flow is to put you into the path of abundance, you truly can't avoid it. Abundance isn't just money. Abundance from the spiritual source means that everything you need is going to be taken care of. This may mean that you will have a great deal of money, that someone else's funds will provide for you, or similar alternatives.

Potentially, we can be on the band/spiral of any and all of those aspects. Whichever choice you make starts the karmic flow. Once you make the commitment to cooperate with Spirit, you will start rising toward this inheritance. The cliché that actions speak louder than words is valid with regard to the spiritual hierarchy. Actions of **A + UL** do move you upward and make your divine inheritance more accessible.

Can you fall? You bet your loving ego, you can fall. And hard. For example, as you're on the way up, you may pass some being who is on the way down. You may mistake that being for God because, in the spiritual world, you will see their brilliance, for they have just come out of the higher realms. The only thing is, *they are on the way down.* You may be so taken with their reflection that you follow them right back down here—here, the land of reflected Light.

How do you avoid that? Tune in. Attune inside. Harmonize with the frequency of Spirit, and you will know whether a force is ascending or descending.

Three Masters

The guardian angels have above them three masters, who direct the teachers. Depending on the population, there are between half a million and five million teachers to each master. Each has an area of the planet with which to deal, going from the realm above the physical up to and including the etheric. These three masters are sometimes referred to as council chiefs; other groups might call them the karmic board. Very few people in the physical body have had access to levels as high as that of the guardian angel group. Jesus, Buddha, Zoroaster, and maybe a few select others had such access.

Many of these beings had a difficult time until around the age of 40, at which time the major karma of the planet, for them, was completed. They were then shifted from the council, the band around you, up to a higher council, and then above that to the teachers or the masters. This is rare. The opportunity is there, but the probability is low. This isn't offered as discouragement; it is just what is. For instance, if we took electricity and put a hot wire carrying 1 watt in your hand, you could hold on to it with a minimum of discomfort. If we turned it up to 50,000 watts, you would fry. That's what you would be trying to do in ascending to the height of the masters.

One of the masters is chosen as the avatar. Above that avatar there is a Logos or God of the planet. That God is still in the negative realms. If an individual chooses great negativity, that can evoke support from the negative aspects of that God. This can manifest in many forms, including possessions (which is another good reason to focus on the positive and get positive support).

The Magic Word

As you sow, so shall you reap, which brings us to the magic word on this planet: attitude. If your attitude is one of conditional loving, then that is what you will get back. If your loving does not go out to your mother-in-law or father-in-law, your boss, your enemy, your friend, and yourself, you are inviting disharmony into your beingness. If you participate in spiritual exercises and go toward the inner kingdom with judgments of others and yourself, you are going there in a state of negativity. This is as though you have given a gold-plated invitation for the negative forces to join you and eat at your table. You'll probably both be "eating crow" for a while.

Once Kal comes to dinner, it's like an old play called *The Man Who Came to Dinner.* It was almost impossible to get rid of him. If you embrace unworthiness or righteousness at someone else's expense and choose the band's power in negativity, you can create your own hell in this very lifetime. Vigilance and awareness are either ignored cliches on your way to hell or positive actions on your way to Soul.

Don't ignore the fact that this spiritual hierarchy I have described operates from the negative (lower) realms of consciousness. The hierarchy of the planet receives its instructions from levels *below* the Soul realm, and that includes the avatar, ascended masters, the Great White Brotherhood, and all the others. They are beautiful, radiant beings, yet their domain is in realms from which reembodiment occurs. They are not in the vibratory frequency of the Soul realm.

To get off this planet, *we do need* the assistance of these masters, guardian angels, avatars, and gods of the planet. To get to the Soul realm, we need the guidance of the Mystical Traveler Consciousness.

Service

Service is the highest form of consciousness in the physical world. When we recognize our love of humanity, we do whatever has to be done to express that love to and with others. That is called service. The service I am talking about is not your occupation. Your vocational expression (for which you are paid) often fulfills the planet's karmic law, which is that by the sweat of your brow you earn your living. That is perfect, but it is not the service I am dealing with here.

Service is an expression of loving in action, with no demand for or expectation of a reward (monetary or otherwise). *Service is its own reward.* Along with that expression there are often side effects, known as joy and upliftment. The person who does service and tries to get publicity for it limits the benefit of the act to their being known for the act. The person who does it in silence, acting in a loving consciousness just to do it—that person builds up the Light, which neutralizes negative karma.

All this theory about service remains theory, unless you try it on for size. The Mystical Traveler often says, "Don't believe me. You don't have to have faith in what I say. Check it out for yourself." The best way to check out the value of service is by being of service to someone or some group that isn't part of your usual domestic or vocational life. Go to a home for the blind and read to them. Go to an old age home and talk to some of the lonely, dear people. Go to a veteran's hospital and play cards with some of the guys there. Go to a children's hospital and just hold a child and tell them stories. Type letters, stuff envelopes, do whatever is required for an organization whose entire existence is based on sharing unconditional loving. Any of these acts is guaranteed to do two things: (1) assist those in need, and (2) lighten and make things easier and more joyful for you and, as a result, more joyful for anyone who comes in contact with you.

Passaging into the upper realms of Spirit takes Light and lightness. When people move into a negative perception of their experiences, they burden themselves with a heavy, gross consciousness that is anchored to this physical level. I have seen people do this in relationship to service. Some have found themselves in a situation of service and have started to feel as though they were in a prison. So, rather than use service as an expression of Light giving, they felt it as a burden to carry.

People often misunderstand the concept of service, not recognizing that it is an active form of moving the spiritual consciousness, which takes place primarily when you serve from the level of positive attitude. Although you could respond, "Oh, I have to help them again," it would serve you better—and who better to serve?—if you expressed the attitude, "Thank God I can be of service again."

Being of service is a matter of doing with no other thought in mind except that of freely doing. The freedom is in serving under any conditions, past conditioned feelings and ego.

The great masters and teachers have come here to serve human beings. They really are the servants, and they recognize that this is a God-granted privilege. They exemplify this by serving in a consciousness of love and joy.

The opportunity to serve comes in areas and at times that you may not expect. Even though it may not be totally convenient for you from this physical level, I suggest you don't reject the opportunity. If you are open to serve,

Spirit will bring forth the way. If it comes forward and you have an attitude of "Well, not that, and I'm busy this weekend," then Spirit will respect you and leave you to your limited serving. You may also be left with your limitations, on many other levels.

Embracing Spirit is a very specific action with proven techniques. One of the keys to opening the door to greater freedom, joy, and abundance on all levels is doing what it takes in the areas of need. The result will be greater love, joy, and freedom *inside* you. Another by-product will be greater joy, love, and freedom *outside* you, in relationships and deeds. You will find that the spiritual energy will permit you to perform tasks far beyond your conditioned capacity in terms of time and accomplishment.

Check it out. Try it. Do it.

Service is not just an altruistic expression of doing it for others. It is a divine expression of doing it for the God-loving force in you.

Call the Garbage Man

Once you participate in the expression of service and s.e.'s, the Traveler will go into all the levels of your beingness, stirring things up; the karmic garbage will become apparent, and the Traveler will take it. *The Traveler* is another name for garbage collector, and, in this spiritual quest, *garbage* is another word for ego, righteousness, judgments, and negativity toward others and self.

The Traveler will not work with you to "clean up your act" unless you ask. Its spiritual contract requires its nature to be non inflictive. You have to ask in s.e.'s and acts of service in order to get the Traveler's support. Because you and the Traveler are one, you will get all the action and support you ask for and can handle, and the fact is that *God* never gives you more than you can handle.

Those who work with the Traveler in true commitment will transcend and be released from this level in this lifetime. Those initiates who may weaken and mistakenly create negative energy through their spiritual expression can take more lifetimes before they get to the heart of God, which is their divine inheritance.

Originally, after the first separation, when energy was expressed in the lower levels away from the Soul realm, the idea was for the karma to be balanced in as few as six lifetimes. The divine plan was ignored, however, and more energy was expressed toward the mind and ego than toward Soul. As a result, the process of balancing karma and returning to the heart of God can now take thousands of existences.

When you die from this level, you can incarnate into another level, such as the causal realm, and it is possible to build karma there before you are reborn back to this earth. Some, however, do come back rapidly. There are those who are confused by the possibility of their Soul incarnating on a level other than Earth. That is because they think of themselves as human beings and figure that all incarnations must be on this planet where human beings reside.

They are mistaken in their approach because the Soul is not a human Soul; it is just a Soul. It *can* take any form. We, in our ego, call it the human Soul, but that's not very accurate. Thinking that our human-being status is supreme is part of the trap of this physical level. If you think this is the only or primary level for your existence, you will continue to create your reembodiment on this level.

If you don't choose to transcend these lower levels with the Traveler now and if you choose not to ask, that's all right, too. Eventually, since your destiny is divine completion, you will ask. It may be 25,000 to 28,000 lifetimes from now, but the time will come. Spirit never seems in a hurry.

The Lord of the Physical Realm

The physical world is under another Lord, called Lucifer or Satan in most Christian religions. His spiritual name is Kal Niranjan. He is the Lord of this world, running it as he wills. There is not a devil in the physical form, for it was not allowed the opportunity to have a body, but there is definitely the energy of Kal, which permeates this planet. This negative energy manifests in thoughts and deeds of individuals and groups.

Hell is similar. It is not a place in the center of the earth, but a state of consciousness. I suggest you don't shrug it off by saying, "Well, if it's just a state of consciousness, I don't have to be concerned." The hellish conditions that have been created from states of consciousness are definitely to be regarded with awareness. Eternal vigilance is a valuable caution. The brutality and unkindness generated on this planet have come from the consciousness of lack, of greed, of lust, of judgment, of self-righteousness, and of ego.

The consciousness of human beings is most powerful. Be aware of what you think, feel, and, particularly, what you say and do. Make the effort to monitor yourself into loving, rather than indulge conditioned negativity. The latter is the condition that people ascribe to the devil, but all the time it was you, opening the door to the forces of Kal Niranjan, the negative ruler of planet Earth.

When Jesus the Christ was here physically, he went into the realm where the Kal power existed and told Kal Niranjan that he could no longer bind the Souls from the Light. Jesus the Christ built a spiritual bridge across the realms for the Souls to return to God. Prior to that time, the negative power (Kal) could "punish" any Soul that turned toward the Light (God). Kal would put them in a place called purgatory for punishment and purification.

Many religions worship Kal, some knowingly, most unknowingly. Kal is extremely powerful and deceitful. The Kal power can affect a most orthodox presentation, from a church to a seemingly self-righteous minister.

This Kal power has all the disincarnate entities under it. The devils and the demons that live in the various realms present themselves as you ascend in your awareness. Some people, when confronted by a gigantic demon, get so frightened that they awaken back in their beds, vowing never to do spiritual exercises again. The Kal force celebrates, having won, because when a person abandons something positive out of fear, they are trapped on this level, Kal Niranjan's domain. Spiritual exercises are the key to transcending the negative realms back to the heart of God.

Your job, from the day you are born, is to get out of here, off planet Earth, and return to the God-realm. This earth is a classroom. When you learn the lessons, you have earned good karma, and then you meet the Mystical Traveler. He starts you working off the karma on the levels above you. You are responsible for this physical level, and, even then, the Traveler will assist you as long as you make the effort in awareness and through positive actions. If you die before you get higher, you do not have to incarnate back again if you are an initiate of the Traveler. Because you are in the ascending line of energy, also called the path of the saints, the science of the Soul, the path of the Travelers, and many other names, you will continue your ascension in Spirit.

Actually, each person is connected to the Traveler. The Traveler activates the Soul and resides in the Soul with you. The Soul is perfect. It exists on all levels. When you do spiritual exercises, you go past the astral, causal, mental, and etheric levels into the Soul of Soul. As you ride the Soul energy in each of these levels, you stay in perfect protection and the Kal power cannot touch you.

The angel Yama is not your enemy. It is Yama's job to make sure that you have learned your lessons. If you have not, you first visit the angel Yama when you die. Yama looks down on your life as your Soul reads all the actions. If you were to see it physically, Yama would appear to be 15 to 20 miles high. This is a form called St. Peter—not the Peter described in the Bible, but the one guarding the first gates of heaven.

When they die, initiates of the Mystical Traveler go through the void into the Soul realm, where Yama *cannot* go. If Kal gets one of the initiates, the Traveler will come and get that Soul and in the process, because of great compassion, will release every other Soul in Kal's domain. Kal does not want that to occur, so he leaves the Traveler's initiates alone.

Kal tried this a while back, and one entire section of the lower astral world was released from bondage because Kal had gone after someone very high in Spirit with the Traveler. The Traveler just went over and got that Soul. Kal protested to the Lord of the fifth (Soul) realm, who is the Mystical Traveler on that level and who told Kal that he knew better than to bother with an initiate. In other words, "Shut up and go to your realm!"

Just because you have now read and thought about the devil, Kal Niranjan, and Yama, I suggest you avoid the "the-devil-made-me-do-it" attitude. Don't give the devil more credit than is due. Most of us do "it" ourselves quite well, thank you. First you get it started with nega-tive thinking, then you feed it with negative fantasies, then you activate it with negative doing, and then you are creating karma by the bucket load. You blame the devil, when all along you were doing it. As it always has been, you are the source. You are the cause and effect. You are the problem and the solution. You are the devil and the good Lord.

Is This Trip Necessary?

Why don't we just avoid all the trouble and travail on planet Earth? Because when we are up in the Spirit world, where everything is seen from a neutral, non-judgmental place, everything looks easy. There is nothing to avoid when we come from a spiritual non-position. From that place, we do not recognize that there are better worlds than this one, in terms of fun. In terms of learning the karmic lessons we have created for ourselves, this world is a master school or a giant trap.

The true magic on this physical level is *attitude*. Once you have the attitude of freedom, you can get above all this and see how funny it is. You can laugh about it from the proper altitude. Then it doesn't hurt and you walk free.

One of the biggest traps is taking everything so terribly seriously. You are serious about being right or wrong, about doing something that might get you in trouble, about passing the exam, getting married, getting divorced, getting married, and raising a family. Relax. The most serious person on this planet still won't get off it alive.

If you do good because good is the loving thing to do, you are doing it the way the Traveler does it. If you do good because you want people to like you, you are doing it the way the Kal power does it. Take your choice. If your choice is not one involved in loving, the Traveler will be illusive. The choice involves loving in every conscious level. Love the person with whom you are in relationship rather than put energy into complaint and what's wrong with them. That means loving them regardless of what they do. It's called unconditional loving. Love thine enemy. Either it'll make them crazy, or a position will change so they will no longer be your enemy. You may even give up a position so that the one who was once an enemy may be converted into a loving friend.

It is possible that in previous lifetimes you were a parent or a child of many of the people you know. If you can be aware of that possibility, you might not be so critical of someone else's behavior.

The thing to realize is that everyone (including you) has a history of deprivation. Making someone wrong for mistakes is like punishing them for their past. There is nothing anyone can do about the past. There is only the present in which we can improve. How do you know you are improving? If you are expressing more joy and acceptance, you are improving in Spirit as on Earth.

Each of us makes mistakes. This is the planet of mistakes. You may be one big mistake on the physical level, a divine mistake, where the erring physical eventually dies and the part that is not a mistake, the part that is perfect and lives perennially, your experienced Soul, joins the perfectly experienced Soul—God.

Is this easy to do in this world? No. If it were easy, you wouldn't be here. If there is one thing you have to learn in this schoolroom of a planet, it's the expression of unconditional loving under difficult conditions. You don't have to love the mistakes people make, but you do have to learn how to love the person and to express caring for them, rather than criticism and righteous judgment.

Do These Karmic Lessons Ever Stop?

When Jesus was asked what his ministry was, he said it was a ministry by example. Such are the karmic lessons offered to each individual. Until we exemplify the lessons of unconditional loving, we have to incarnate back to this realm—over and over and, if necessary, over a thousand or more lifetimes again.

Being born and dying on this planet are never mistakes. They are always part of the divine plan of learning. Even premature births and deaths are part of that plan. A person may finish 99 percent of their karma and then die. When they come back, they have to finish only 1 percent, and that 1 percent may be accomplished in the mother's womb. There is no need to go further, so the Soul pulls back, and the child is part of the still-birth process. This may cause a potential mother to grieve, and that's understandable. If you could only get the altitude, however, you would have joy in your heart, knowing that another being has completed their karma and has gone back to God.

When a being's work is finished—in the womb or in two days, a month, a year, or 88 years—so be it. No being belongs to us. Every child is a child of God, regardless of age.

Returning to God takes awareness, commitment, and practice. Because the trip is sometimes arduous, it also requires loving support that has the power of Spirit within it. The Traveler provides that support. Your expression in spiritual exercises permits that support to enter where needed. S.e.'s are simultaneously an act of practice and support, giving and calling on the divine energy within you.

Do you want to transcend these negative levels? Do you want to eliminate the karma you embodied with on this planet? You do it by going inside to build the spiritual energy. When some of the karma comes forward, the spiritual energy burns up the seeds of the karma, and then you don't have to participate in negative karmic lessons. You can go on in loving balance, without eating of the karmic seed. It is gone.

Practice doing spiritual exercises and you can eventually lift through each realm, *in awareness,* directly into Soul. It's not a theory. It's a proven technique validated by thousands of people who have been doing s.e.'s for years. Practice spiritual exercises, practice loving—because love is the essence of Soul.

This is not new information. There has always been a way out. God has never abandoned us. God is right here, right now. It's we who have been blind enough to move away, but we can move back. When Jesus said, "Believe also in me,"[9] he didn't mean just himself. He also meant the I AM that is God. Now you don't even have to believe. Belief without validation is often a flimsy structure. Even with Jesus, at the end of his mortal life, the disciples who operated only on belief all ran away. All but one, John the Beloved. Jesus, however, did not judge his disciples for the mistakes they made. No, he came back and took those who ran because they were initiates of the Master Traveler, Jesus the Christ.

9. John 14:1, Revised Standard Version

Initiation

The Mystical Traveler usually doesn't initiate people into the energy on the causal level until *after two years of study* because initiation requires more than belief. After a person studies the Soul Awareness Discourses for at least two years, practices s.e.'s for two years, expresses in service for two years (to self, family, loved ones, and individuals and groups who benefit from assistance), then they know empirically whether they want to participate in the Traveler's divine line of transcendence. During those two years the person is traveling in Spirit, in the inner realms, working out karma under the guidance of the Traveler or his agent, which may be an ascended master or a member of the Great White Brotherhood or one of the other thousand brotherhoods.

Before you are physically initiated by a member of the Traveler's staff (who is commissioned by the Traveler to do this), you have already been initiated spiritually. You may not remember it, but you may intuit that experience because you are usually the one who writes the letter requesting the initiation. In the physical initiation, you are told the name of the Lord of the realm above and you are touched in places on the head that are psychic centers, which anchors the energy. As you repeat the name of the Lord, it goes through your body, and you are connected to the divine energy of the next realm. You keep the connection by repeating the Lord's name in a loving consciousness. Doing that is called spiritual exercises.

As mentioned previously, there is a sound and color on each level. As you listen, you can sometimes hear the Sound Current of the level on which you are traveling.

Many times you will not hear or see anything, but that does not invalidate the spiritual experience.

As you are working off karma by chanting your initiatory tones and living a life committed to the process of unconditional loving and service, you may yet fall into traps. When you get your next level of initiation, you may think, "There. I did it. I am now finished with all that emotional karma of the causal realm. I am now a mental initiate!" Be careful that you do not permit a spiritual move to be attached to pride, which is attached to ego, which is attached to a fall. Regardless of level of initiation, no one on the planet is exempt from the negative energy pressure, which is Kal's inner gravity of this world.

You can take pleasure from the fact that you have evolved to the next level, the kind of pleasure that knows you earned it on some level. If you take ego-pleasure, however, you may be stuck in that place, which means dealing with the causal level on the mental realm. Just regard your initiation as a spiritual report card, validating that you are doing something right on the inner realms.

Initiation to the next level does not mean that you completed all the karma of the realms below. It just means that your work created the hole that got you through to where the Soul is ready for the experiences of the next level. The Traveler will push/pull you through that hole, as long as you create that tiny opening. You can go through the eye of a needle, if need be, as long as you do your part.

When you get initiated to the Soul level, it's easy to come down and work out karma through the lower levels, because the Soul does not accrue karma. None of the garbage created from the etheric down to the physical can go into the Soul level, so it drops off like beads of sweat in a sauna. By the time you dive into the ocean of divine love and mercy, you are clean—in Soul.

To be redundant, the process that gets you there is spiritual exercises and service. This needs repeating because you may have been repeating lifetime after lifetime of karmic expressions. By the act of reading this, you can be indicating that you are interested in completing your karma this lifetime.

After you have participated in enough spiritual exercises, you are so full of Light that you project it ahead of you. This permits you to have the vision to avoid the pitfalls of negative conditioning because with the spiritual Light comes clarity of vision. The by-product of clarity is loving—not the type of loving that is the romantic attachment of the movies, but the eternal, ascending, God-like loving.

It's like turning on the car lights to illuminate what is ahead. If you run down the battery, the lights get dimmer and dimmer until you can barely see the hole in the road that's just ahead. Yet running the car charges the battery. That's exactly what spiritual exercises do. The more you do, the more energy you create, the more spiritual Light units you put in the "bank" for when you need an especially large "withdrawal" for support during a particular learning time.

Light units and Light columns are the form on which the pure energy from the God sources comes in. Many initiates of the Traveler actually plant Light columns around the planet. These Light columns are anywhere from 50 feet to 5,000 miles wide. They are like great generator stations that accumulate Light energy. These Light columns channel the pure energy that is Spirit. People who come into contact with this feel that they have come onto sacred and holy ground.

Ministers in MSIA plant Light columns as part of their ministry, and it isn't complicated to do. It is most effectively done while a person is physically standing in the area. They visualize a white Light coming down through them. Then it will appear, that is, if the minister has been consistent in doing spiritual exercises. One can call on the Light, and it may or may not come in, depending upon the spiritual attunement of the one calling it in. Spiritual exercises are the tuning fork for Spirit and Light.

Light

Don't let your appetite for spiritual salvation push you toward getting just the *information* rather than the *experience*. There are some who will read every book and listen to every seminar tape in order to learn about the Light. Mental information will not give you the experience. In fact, if you base your approach on information received only in the mental area, you are ripe for becoming an automaton, perfect for operating your life on what someone says rather than on your experience. If you have your own experience, no one can take that away from you. They can challenge you, but you don't even have to defend yourself because you know, by experience, what is so for you.

You do not receive the experience of Light before you are ready for it. There are some who may push for it—"I'm ready now; I know it"—and they may discover that they actually aren't ready when the energy backs up on them. If Spirit really poured it on the way people ask, some might be burned to a crisp.

You must first learn to traverse the astral realm in Soul consciousness and then move into the causal realm, step by spiritual step, in order to receive the Light's power. The higher you get, the more refined the quality of Light and Sound becomes. In that experience, you will find yourself not so much seeking the Light as creating experiences in which you give and receive the Light. If you want success in your spiritual quest, become one who moves, does, becomes, and experiences. This is the foundation of all consciousness expansion.

By doing, you expand on the gift of God that is already within, and thus comes the experience. Theory is interesting, and intellectual information may be valuable if you use it to improve behavior so that the experience becomes one of neutrality and unconditional loving. Ultimately, what is important is your own experience.

In the Bible, the rod and staff[10] are symbols of Sound (the rod of power) and Light (the staff that sustains all things). Light is part of the essence of spirituality, and it has an inner and an outer quality. The inner quality is what we call a spiritual Light, and the outer quality is what we call a magnetic Light.

Can you live in the spiritual Light all the time? On this planet, most of your time is spent within the electromagnetic Light of the lower realms. The physical body is not equipped to live in the spiritual Light all the time; it could not hold the energy patterns.

The Mystical Traveler has the ability to work with you individually, teaching you how to work with the Light through the lower, magnetic realms of Light until you have established yourself in the Soul realm.

When you move into Soul consciousness and live continuously in that, you then, of course, live continuously in the spiritual Light. So, even on this physically structured level, you can still move your consciousness past physical limitations into the Soul level, which permits you to live—in essence—in the spiritual Light as much and as often as you create that experience.

The magnetic Light functions in the levels below the Soul level, which are in the negative energy field. The Soul resides on each negative level by coming in from the positive realms on the magnetic Light. So, in essence, when you are functioning in the realms from the physical through the etheric, you get the benefit of both the magnetic Light and the spiritual Light. When you learn how

10. Psalm 23:4

to utilize and balance the effect of the two, you can experience cosmic consciousness on the level of the physical world. That is the key to enlightenment.

This process is also practical on this level. When you have connected to the apex of the two Lights, little and large miracles continually manifest. You will find parking places waiting for you on the busiest blocks, you'll receive a tax refund just when you are short of money, or you might be gifted with a ticket to an event that is seemingly sold-out. Those are just some of the enjoyable residuals of this spiritual balance. They are not the goal, however. If you make earth-level miracles the goal, you are trapped.

In MSIA we do not focus on creating that perfect apex on the physical level. That may happen occasionally, but we are essentially working toward moving from the physical up to the Soul realm, rather than making everything perfect on this planet of seeming limitations. In fact, in MSIA we attempt to have at least one-half degree of difference between the magnetic Light and the spiritual Light. We want them to be off a little because the magnetic Light is designed to produce in this world as we learn, gain, grow, take risks, succeed, fail, get up, and go on again. That's part of the design.

Although the spiritual Light can be used on this physical level, it is not essentially designed to transform this brief earthly existence (although that is possible). It is an exquisite energy on the Soul path home.

If a person stands in a pulpit, pounding a book and telling you all about the spiritual demands, with no consideration for the karmic learning designs of this planet, they're often the first to sneak out behind the church and violate the credos they have so assertively laid down.

It is important to progress in this world and handle the challenges responsibly. With this commitment, we can bring the spiritual energies down into this world and start cleaning up the pollution on the physical and on the inner worlds of the astral, causal, mental, and etheric. We have a job to do as co-creators with God. Spiritual and physical ecology are totally compatible.

When you participate in a Light initiation, there are times when you move to a place in your inner awareness where the spiritual and magnetic Lights do come together. At those times of connection, you may be out of the body traveling and may have moments of pure enlightenment so brilliant that your body may shake, you may fall on the floor, or you may get stigmata. All sorts of phenomena may occur. When those forces come together, disappearances can also take place, as they have when the forces have converged regularly in certain physical areas on the planet.

Again, I caution you that this is information to be filed so that if one of these experiences happens to you, you'll be able to say, "Ah, so that's what I'm experiencing." This is not a carrot for you to chase. If you do, you will be the donkey chasing a carrot eternally dangled from a stick in front of it (and you're holding the stick), rather than the human being experiencing the lessons for the Soul. Don't go after the phenomena as a goal, or you may very well get what you want. Do you know what you'll have then? Phenomena. The icing is not the cake. Focus on the Soul realm in essence, rather than on the occasional accoutrements of Spirit.

Inside Out

Everything I have shared in this book is available to you as working knowledge—and *you* have to work it. The gift of God in the form of truths is of value only if you accept, embrace, and activate it. I am just a messenger. The message is of God.

There is not the seeming separation between you, the messenger, the message, and God. Once you awaken, you will realize that all of these are yours for the loving. You are Prince Charming and Sleeping Beauty, awaiting the kiss that awakens. You are also the one who must kiss with the lips of your loving heart, choosing to know the truth. It takes great courage to see the face of God.

The truth can express itself in every and any form. You can experience the truth on word levels, artistic levels, relationship levels, financial levels, vocational levels, and spiritual levels.

To avail yourself of these truths—and they shall be self-evident—you must immerse yourself in the practices that bring to you the brilliant awareness, the sights and sounds of the inner realms. When you come from the realms of Spirit, you will recognize truth when you see it, when you hear it, and when you feel it, as an experience of Light. It will also recognize you, as Light recognizes Light.

You don't have to look for heaven to show itself in the skies; just look in the eyes of a little child and you'll see heaven. You don't have to see the waters part to validate the truth; just assist some needful person and you'll experience your loving beyond your expectations.

See and hear from the inner realms and you will know that the simple truths, when applied, can create a life of joy and fulfillment on this level all the way up to the Soul realm.

Here are some of the truths that I hear:

Sin is only ignorance.

The greatest sin is fear.

The most exquisite moment is now.

The greatest person is the one who does not force you to change.

The most dangerous liars are those who lie to themselves.

The most joyful play is the work of service.

Comfort is knowing you have done your work well.

The only mistake is giving up.

The only stumbling block is your ego.

The only loss is when you lose your enthusiasm.

The greatest thing is love.

These truths are the teachings of God, not humans. There is no ego in these teachings. Do they work? Of course, but on one condition, that is, when you give up *your* conditioned process and accept the unconditioned process of God. Unconditionally. At that point, there is nothing you have to do because the process will work through you, and it shall be God speaking through you as you.

Within that, there is the subtle trap of making the mistake that *you* are GOD. In you is God, and you are not God. Only God is God. If you claim that you are God and define the Light as you in your form, the illusion is but a trapdoor to your fall. Your ego is the trigger. Reembodiment and karma are the lessons.

When you permit the process of God to work through you, you have opened the way to the cure for depression, dis-ease, and all negative conditions. Notice that I said you have opened the way. As with all things on this physical level, you have to work the cure for it to have effect. Instead of concentrating on the effect and asking God to treat the dis-ease, *you open to the cure by changing the cause.* You have to demonstrate the ability to let go of those foods, those relationships, those lusts, and those emotional outbursts that contribute to illness. In that act of letting go, you permit God to cooperate in your healing.

It is no mistake that the organization that channels the teachings of the Mystical Traveler Consciousness is called the Movement of Spiritual Inner *Awareness.* You must develop your awareness if you are to serve yourself for your highest good. Once you are aware, you can watch. Then you can be vigilant. For, as a man with ulcers knows that fried food isn't good for him, so does a spiritually aware person know what is supportive in Spirit and what isn't. You know by reaching into the inner realms to listen and see. Look before you leap. Yes, look inside before you leap outside. Inside, you can know the truth about every situation, circumstance, and relationship if you but have the courage to look and listen.

There will be times when you get specific guidance. It can be as prosaic as "no more coffee." If you ignore this or dissipate the energy by thinking, "Well, I'll just have three cups today instead of my normal six," you may be distancing yourself from Spirit. Spirit gives, and a receiver must then activate the information. If the receiver ignores the gift of Spirit, there are 4.5 billion other Souls in need of direct input from Spirit. If you ask for assistance and guidance from Spirit, then use it. In other words, watch what you ask for because you just might get it.

In Search of Security

Earlier, I said that forgiveness is a key to spiritual growth. There is an even more advanced action, that of awareness. Yes, awareness is an action when used appropriately. When you are aware that this planet is the land of karmic lessons, when you are aware that each person progresses at his or her own rate, when you are aware that the mistakes others make are more painful to them than anyone else, then, in your awareness, you will hold for them. You will never take away your love because of something they do or don't do. So, if there is one thing you learn from this book, learn this:

**There is never a good enough reason
to take away your love.**

Part of awareness is to have enough patience with everyone (including yourself) during the sometimes-difficult learning experiences. That is the *only* reason we are here: to learn. It's difficult only because we often focus on the impossible. Most people are involved in the quest for that thing (or, with most, those things) that will make this world secure for them: that relationship, that amount of money, that job; then it becomes that divorce, that new job, that new investment—anything that will make things seem secure. This is the impossible dream, strictly from the astral world, because you can never have enough money, sex, marriages, possessions, drugs, or jobs to secure your life on this level for more than a few metaphorical minutes. Diabolical?

Sure, it is, but guess who's the Lord of this realm? None other than the prince of the diabolical, Kal Niranjan. By design, if you stick to this physical level, you have the appetite for more, and Kal laughs, knowing there will never be enough (more) to satisfy the more-lust.

I read about a man who won a lottery that amounted to $12 million. An incredible amount, and tax-free, too. A friend of mine envied him and said, "Oh, dear God, if it were only me. I wouldn't have to worry for the rest of my life." Not less than three weeks later, I read that the winner had died of a heart attack. My friend was right. The lottery winner didn't have to worry for the rest of his life, short as it was.

What's the cure for this impossible paradox? It's called getting off the planet. Do you have to wait until you die? I suggest you don't. I suggest you live this life fully, enjoyably, with humor, and with all the goods that are enjoyable to you, as long as you keep your focus where the eternal security is: the Soul realm, God.

Information or the Lesson

Some say that people are punished for their sins. We are actually punished *by* our sins. The sin of ignorance, or lack of awareness, punishes the person. Some think that death is punishment, but most people are not so lucky. They will get their karmic lessons right here, alive and not well. Express yourself in lust, and lust will turn around and beat you up on this level. Then you may pray to the gods to cure you of herpes, but all Spirit can do is respect your action of lust and permit you the learnings available in the lesson called herpes. In some cases you may implore Spirit to help you get past your impotency or frigidity. Just know that the lords of karma will hold forth, permitting you the lesson of the experience. It would be wiser to pray for guidance before you indulge yourself than to beseech the gods to relieve you of your karma. Spirit doesn't always work that way.

If you recognize that, stop berating the gods, and embrace your own knowledge, you are on the way to the release. Once you accept the lessons, they become the information. With that attitude, you gain the altitude for release of karma, and, once again, you are on the passage to the upper realms.

Part of acceptance is handling the karmic infliction you created. You do this not by saying, "It's my karma" and then forgetting it in a posed divine acceptance, but by handling the situation on this level through divine acceptance. That includes proper self-care in the forms of exercise and diet. That includes getting direction and assistance from those who are trained to give that.

Spirit works through medical doctors and medicine, as well as chiropractors, acupuncturists, homeopathic remedies, and herbs. Do what you can on this physical level by handling your physical problems. Don't go to the doctor for a miracle cure, particularly if you have created physical karma for yourself. Go to the doctor for what they can do, that is, for assistance, comforting, intelligent advice, and easing of symptoms. When you come down to it, the doctor treats the effects of the cause. It is you who must handle the cure by seeing the cause. Fasting one day and eating chocolate cake the next may be a difficult way to do it. Change your habits for your betterment. When your behavior has changed, you'll know you have learned. It is then that the cure is in effect.

Do what you can on the spiritual levels through s.e.'s and service, and do what you can on the other levels by doing it in loving. Don't give up on yourself and don't give up on God because God never gives up on you. Not only do what the doctor suggests but do what Spirit suggests. You will hear and see the direction of Spirit in the inner realms if you have been practicing.

If you haven't practiced enough, you can start now because as long as we're in a physical body, no one, no body, is exempt from the negative influences. So you may as well start putting Light units in the bank, now. You may need a sudden withdrawal for that rainy karmic day, and if you don't, how marvelous. You can use all the Light you have stored for the benefit of others, on your way home to God.

Check It Out

When we go inside and do hear direction, it may come from two different sources. One of these locations is on the right or in the center of the spiritual eye. This will be the merciful God and the Traveler. The other will come from the left and will be the Kal force or negative power. How will you know the difference or value of the direction? If you're an initiate, just chant your tone. If the direction is from a negative source, the energy will dissipate, and if it is from a positive source, it will hold up.

Then, on every level, check it out. If you hear an inner voice saying, "Enter that 10-K run tomorrow," you might check it out with your simple knowing.

Have you been running and training?

(Not for three years.)

What's the longest distance you ran during the last six months?

(Just down the block for the bus.)

Compute all that information and what do you get? If you enter that 10-K race, you may suffer from exhaustion and dehydration, go into a coma, and possibly die.

Therefore, the next time you hear that voice say, "Enter the 10-K," just tell it, "You run. I'm not in shape." In other words, don't romanticize and distort Spirit beyond your intelligence. Spirit is all-intelligence and all-knowing and is totally practical on all levels. Make sure you check out everything to support your hearing on these levels. The Spirit may be telling you something as simple as "do more physical activity."

When you hear negative direction, including input giving you the feeling that you may be disconnected from Spirit, you can handle it simply by doing that which supports you. You could use the 10-K advice to support you by realizing you are out of shape and starting to exercise at the gym every night. If the negative force tries to convince you that Spirit and you are no longer one, sit down, call in the Light, and start chanting. In time, you will experience your spiritual connection.

The truth is that Spirit never disconnects anyone. Only when beings give their energy to the Kal force do they disconnect themselves from Spirit. Even then, they can reconnect themselves. This may take devotedly doing spiritual exercises over a long period of time. It is worth it, however, because it is the cure for karma—not a temporary manifestation but a cure. When we have crossed the bridge from the negative binds to the Soul, we have chosen to be karmically free.

Travelers have essentially used three actions as part of developing the inner hearing (also known as the spiritual awareness). *One* action is making spiritual information available and accessible to those who make the commitment to Soul transcendence. During this time, a form of this information is the Soul Awareness Discourses, which carry the awakening energy. *Another* action is offering live or taped seminars, where the karma is released (satsang). If these two don't work, there is a *third*, in which the person has the karmic opportunity to handle adversity and to learn, love, accept, and transcend.

This last can be presented in the form of losing a job or a mate or, perhaps, experiencing an illness that turns the person more toward God. If none works to release the karma, the person will once again reembody; eventually, however, the person will relate to this physical place from the inside out.

Use or Abuse of Energy

On our upward path of releasing karma, we need to use our energy to our advantage. It's for our highest good to be ecological with the one thing we can waste: our energy. It takes a great deal of energy to transcend these lower levels into the positive realms. Use it wisely because you are gifted with a finite amount.

On the physical level the body drains the most negative energy through the two lowest cavities, which are called the eliminative and reproductive organs. If we abuse the energy release of those levels, we can create an energy leak. Our precious energy, which could be used for ascendance, can leak out through emotionalizing or fantasizing.

Spiritual exercises build up the reservoir of energy inside you. Then you choose whether to use that energy to Soul travel out of the body or release it through sexual activity. Either way, the same kind of energy is used. When you don't use the energy for your highest good, you can experience depression, irritation, and anxiety. I am not suggesting that you should avoid the sexual expression. In loving, this expression can be enriching; in lusting, depleting.

One of the quickest ways to release this energy is through masturbation. Instead of saving and containing that seed energy for Spirit, you release it within the shortcomings of the human form. If you're married and still involved in masturbation, you are limiting your expression and energy and are releasing it within a negative field. If you make love with your partner in loving, the energy can be recycled to you through tender loving.

You are responsible for the appropriate use of your spiritual energy. You have to awaken your sight in order to get direction. Then you have to choose to go in the direction of your limitless sight, rather than turn away to the direction of your limitations. You are the co-creator. If you do not do it, it may not get done.

All the information shared in this book, in your life, in all your existence, has always been available in various forms of consciousness on this planet. These levels of consciousness are open books when you develop the inner sight to read them.

If you mock up inner vision and use the information I have offered as validation, it will work as well as a mock-up Porsche with a Volkswagon engine. You don't have to mock up or create anything in this world. The only thing you might choose to do is continually recreate your choice of doing what it takes to keep awakening. Enter into this process with joy, with a sense of completeness. Completeness, because that will permit you to use all your energy for the moment at hand, here and now.

If you leave incomplete projects to abound, they "sting" the unconscious and drag on you. You may be unaware of the cause, but the effect will be your walking around feeling heavy, with the low-energy blues. Even after you sleep like the dead for ten hours, you'll still think you need a great deal of sleep. It's called the karma of incompletions.

Be good to yourself. If you feel a sense of discomfort with some expression, take that inner guidance as a warning light. Check it out, clear it out, and then do what feels clear to do—not clear from the place of ego or emotional attachment, but clear from that place you have cleaned up inside you as a Soul source, that place inside you that *is* integrity, that place of inner seeing that knows whether an action or inaction is involved in loving. If loving isn't involved in the action, the action is not from the Soul.

Don't romanticize the Soul essence. Wiping a child's nose can be a Soul-source action. Avoiding expressions that might hurt someone might be an empathic action, and saying no may sometimes be a loving expression. When you are involved in an unconditional loving action, you are involved in Soul.

Use your energy to go inside where you have developed your inner sight. Look with the eyes of the Beloved. The Beloved isn't just the Christ or the Traveler or God. The Beloved is You.

Where is God?

Throughout this book, as well as throughout our lives, the *only issue* is returning home to God. The only pure motive is the love of God, and God *can be* found in everything and every one.

God has been called many things by many people. Yet, there is but one God. Some call it Allah or Krishna, and others call it Christ. People often attempt to isolate God within their cultural or religious vocabulary definition. They try to own God, making God their private domain, available to others on a membership-only basis, the dues being anything from worshiping according to a specific doctrine to paying specified amounts of money to a church. This purportedly ensures that the church and its head will pray for you, which guarantees salvation, since they supposedly have a private line to God. Yet, there is but one God.

The "one God" turns away no loving Souls. The one God is not concerned with doctrine, physical rules of behavior that change from generation to generation, or definitions. God answers to any name, as long as it is said in loving.

People have tried so many techniques and approaches and rules and regulations to get to God. Loving is the approach that works.

You may seek out a so-called illuminated being—a guru, a rishi, a sage, a sadhu—and ask that being to show you God. If that being is coming from a place of integrity, they will not show you God, except perhaps with a mirror. They will, however, point a way, perhaps again with a mirror. For the journey starts with you, inside you, and it completes with you because God dwells not only in the heavens above but within you, where some of the heavens also exist.

You take that inner journey yourself. There are few beings who can deliver God to you. You must have the experience of God for yourself.

That is why the Movement of Spiritual Inner Awareness is such a nonrestrictive, eclectic organization. MSIA accepts any and every method of finding God, as long as it includes unconditional loving as an integral part of the expression. If that approach does not include loving, we are not doing that approach.

There are some beings on the planet who have developed different levels of awareness and who demonstrate this. You may be one of them, but you are still here on this earth plane. Be cautious and do not get caught up in the illusion that we sometimes perpetrate on ourselves and others; namely, the glamour of progress, the ego that boasts of how spiritual we are, the mouth that shares how knowledgeable and great we are. This is still the land of reflected light. From this level, we see only by reflection, not by direct Light. We do not see God from this level except by reflection, regardless of how much praise and adoration is offered.

If seen from the inner realms, however, God can be seen everywhere in all things. Those who are attuned to the rarity of Spirit will exemplify the godliness of their beingness in the doing. Their actions, their being, their presence will emanate Spirit. Words, garlands, dress, and performance are, perhaps, the accoutrements of a star, but they are not necessarily the acts of Spirit.

When I talk about God, I am referring to the God of your heart. That is where the angels come to minister to you. These are not metaphorical angels, but real, high-frequency forces with a specific purpose. You can see them, you can intuit them, you can experience them when you look within *from* within.

If you are looking to the outer world as your source of learning, you may learn worldly things, but you will not necessarily experience the unfoldment that leads you to the inner realms of God. From that worldly vantage point, your sensitivities can become so grossly encapsulated that you may not have the ability to discern the vibratory frequency of a healing angel visiting your beingness. You will not know when an answer to your prayers is present because your antennae have been covered up with layers of worldly matters.

It seems to be a paradox that somewhere within the physical form is the sacredness, the holy temple, the residence of God. To get the keys, you have to go within. After reading this book, you may be aware of some of the techniques that facilitate that inner journey. Now it is up to you to do those things that permit you to touch into the kingdom of God.

When you do, it may be so glorious that you may once again embrace your ego, chanting to the world, "I am God." That is close, but not exact. Neither a man nor a woman is God; they are just an extension of God in the process of realizing this. God is an action inside each of us. We can deny it, but we will still be an action in the process of God-realization. The denial can create difficulty and possibly extend the time of the process by lifetimes, but God will still be part of it, just as my hand is part of my body. To deny my hand would be foolish. To deny yourself as part of God would be not only foolish but unnecessarily painful.

When we say, "Father-Mother-God, thy will is done," we are simply accepting what is, rather than placing energy into the denial that tempts us on this physical plane. Not only is it appropriate but it creates greater reception when we affirm that in Light, God is all, in Spirit eternal.

This is not just a spiritual cliché to rush through as a morning prayer so that you can then get on with your life. Your life *is* the frequency of the prayer. The expression of it, from your inner sounds, is a recognition evoking awareness of the Light. This is an action calling on the source of love, the divinity within each of us. It is like training to be a long-distance runner. Each day, you run a little more, and each day, because of the training, you are capable of running a little more. Similarly, each time you call on the Light as a source of your beingness, you increase the Light's amplitude and your ability to receive of it.

You don't have to wait until you die to claim the grace of God. You can have the joy here and now, if, in awareness, you awaken to the inner sight and know that God's will is done on Earth as in heaven. With love, all things are known. That includes successful and happy relationships in marriage, in work, in finances, in service, in God.

Is Love a Concept
or an Action?

With the mind, only the surface of things is known.
The mind looks with eyes that see reflections. The more
you revere the mind, the greater are the possibilities of
your being blinded and bound by its reflection. Don't worship the mind. Worshiping the mind is a form of lower-level
cannibalism because it is actually the mind worshiping itself and, eventually, eating of its own self-producing karma.
When this happens, you have to go along with the mind
because you created, promoted, or allowed this action.

In the mind, love is a concept.
In the heart, love is an action.

Love within the spiritual heart. Then you are able to go
beyond the surface. You will see and hear beyond the pro-
tective facade of worldly distractions. Come from the inner
heart and you will be able to get to that which is causing all
things. You will be privy to the sacred esoteric teachings of
the inner Light and will get the powerful guidance of the
Light of the radiant one we call the Beloved.

When you walk with the Beloved, you walk in the
sanctuary of the consciousness of Spirit. Respect for that
which is within is one of the prime requisites for taking
the inner journey and for receiving the guidance of the
masters who shall accompany you.

Many people hold hostility toward this journey and
those who are committed to the inner travels. The hostility is a result of the fear of the unknown. Many people
choose the comfort of familiarity, even if it is negative,
oppressive, and painful. Because they know it, they will
choose the security of negative familiarity. Yet the security

rapidly dissolves as familiarity breeds contempt and as contempt then breeds destruction. From destruction come additional karmic opportunities on this learning plane, which are sometimes called physical disabilities and other lifetimes in any form that will contribute to the learning, from a beggar in India to a leper in Africa to exactly what you are today. In a previous existence, you may have turned away from the higher teachings and taken comfort in the familiar, so here you are—again.

Each Soul that steps onto the path of spiritual unfoldment will, in time, come into the action of truth. In recognition of this, I suggest that we give up allegiance to labels defining spiritual pursuit; I suggest we let go of any behavioral criteria we demanded in the name of Spirit. Leave spiritual matters to Spirit. All we have to do is develop our ability to tune in to the frequency of Spirit for ourselves. We in MSIA can offer a method that we use as a way that works for us, but don't get attached to it as *the* way. Don't insist that anyone else do it your way. Within Spirit, as long as loving is involved, that is a way that works.

Recognize that part of being human is to make mistakes. If you judge and berate yourself, you are cooperating with the work of the negative forces. If you permit yourself the foibles of being a human being—errors, stupid choices, occasional emotional reactions and actions, thoughts that tempt you away from your spiritual heart—you will still be close to God. Accept them all as part of the physical-astral-causal-mental-etheric package, remembering that you are a spiritual being on the way home to God. Those negative emotions, those aches and pains, and those thoughts of separation are all part of the process. Yes, God is "in" them, too. That is how you bypass the actions of negativity. Recognizing them, say, "Hello, negativity," and embrace the God of Light that is there, letting that Light lead you to the *right* as you leave the conditioning on the *left*—not with anger or judgment, but in awareness that this, too, shall pass.

Who's Minding the Store?

If God is in there, where did the negativity and pain come from? Again, from *your* dear old mind and ego. They have created the illusions that we perpetrate on ourselves, which produces the negativity and disillusionment. The mind will change itself a thousand times in order to stay in charge. When you are in confusion, the mind reigns. The mind will change the words, the rules, and the frames of reference as often as it can, in order to keep you in bondage and itself as the apparent master.

Do you remember when sexual intercourse was condoned only for married couples, and anyone else who engaged in sex was considered immoral? Then times changed and sexual intercourse became acceptable between two consenting adults. Then women and men became aware that there wasn't equal consideration in terms of orgasms. Then men became sex objects as well as women. That's called equality in hell because after that came dissatisfaction and the feeling that the sexual expression was no longer meaningful. Once again, the mind reigns supreme and feeds off confusion.

It takes the heart to bypass the mind and say, "I know better." It takes the heart to say that lovemaking has to do with making love. To make love in the act of sexual intercourse is to be with someone who is loved and is being love. Intercourse without loving can leave you lonely seconds after the orgasm you fought so hard for and felt yourself to be entitled to.

When you come from the heart, however, loving is loving. Then every touch is that expression, regardless of how long you last or how long it takes, because the loving experience outlasts the physical expression.

Don't be a traditionalist and let the mind mind the store. Be a spiritual pioneer and let the actions of the heart (wisdom) lead the way.

Sometimes the heart action will change social mores and move a people from a hypocritical belief to an action of integrity. How will you know? See and hear from the inner realms of Spirit.

In Spirit there is no confusion. There just is. When you are clear, you are in loving. In fact, loving is a by-product of clarity.

Choose the Me in You

I emphasize not going with words as a deterrent to Spirit or as a substitute for action toward Spirit. Then why use words at all? Because, while we share the inexactitude of words, there is a subtextual frequency that is saying, "Open sesame." Only, if you hear with the ears of your heart, you'll realize it says, "Open, says me."

At that point, when the me in you takes responsibility, you are in charge. You can change any condition, action, or reaction in your life because you have now chosen the me-Source, the I AM. It is at this point, if you listen, that you can hear the angels sing and chant in celebration as you enter into your own resurrection. You burgeon like a blossom in spring. Your creativity will flow from deep within. You will resonate from centers so deep within your beauty that you had not known they existed. You will look for a word, a vocabulary expression, and all that will come close is a three-letter word. Joy. Joy. Joy.

We are all dwellers on this threshold into our oneness. Now is our opportunity to cease being the effect and to become the cause. We now have the moment in which we can simultaneously be the knower, the experience, and the destination all within ourselves.

The greatest secret is that the journey is already over before it has begun. You are already there. That one for whom you seek is already present. Why is this a secret? Because so few claim it. Do you? With your next breath?

Are you willing to bypass the limitation of words, of misinterpreting who you are by labeling yourself as bad, or guilty, or frightened, or unworthy? Are you ready to align yourself with God, who always finds you worthy of unconditional loving? Are you courageous enough to know what you know?

Before we came into this embodiment, we committed to becoming aware and to using this level as a springboard into God consciousness, leaving this land of reflected Light and entering into ultimates.

If you embrace this knowing, the path of devotion is actually quite easy because you are then devoted to yourself—not in selfishness but in selflessness, not to the personality or the I of the ego but to the I of the I AM, of God.

In the Movement of Spiritual Inner Awareness, there is a term I use at the end of seminars. It is a gentle reminder of satsang. It is part of the celestial energies in perfect harmonic balance made into words. The statement is simple. It means that we are to reap the benefits and know them as our co-creation. It implies that our task is to know the experience of this phrase:

The blessings already are.

Baruch Bashan

Chart of the Realms

REALM	SOUND	COLOR
POSTIVE REALMS (Spirit) (Spiritual Light)	(Not Verbalized)	(Not Verbalized)
GOD		
27 Levels	HU Thousand violins Angels singing Summer breeze through the willow trees	Clear Pale Gold Light Gold
SOUL	Haunting flutelike sound	Gold
NEGATIVE REALMS (Reembodiment levels) (Magnetic Light) (Karmic Board)	*Cosmic Mirror*	
ETHERIC *(Unconscious)*	Buzzing Bee or buzzing fly	Purple
MENTAL *(Mind)*	Running water or babbling brook	Blue
CAUSAL *(Emotions)* *(Karma)*	Tinkling bells	Orange
ASTRAL *(Imagination)*	Surf/waves	Pink
PHYSICAL *(Conscious self)* *(Physical body)*	Thunder; heart beat	Green

Rukmini canal

Subconscious
Unconscious
Habits
Addictions
Obsessions
Compulsions

(Note: High selves and basic selves may come from any level.)

SPIRIT

GOD

Path of the Mystical Traveler

SOUL

COSMIC MIRROR

Rukmini
Canal

ASTRAL   CAUSAL   MENTAL   ETHERIC   SOUL

ETHERIC

MENTAL

CAUSAL

ASTRAL

PHYSICAL

Glossary

Akashic records. The record of all the experiences of each individual. Also known as the karmic records. Most are kept in the causal realm.

Ani-Hu. A variation of the HU chant. An invocation to the supreme God, with an added dimension calling forth the essence of empathy.

Astral realm. The realm above the physical. The realm of the imagination. Intertwines with the physical as a vibratory rate.

Aura balance. An MSIA service. A technique to clean and strengthen the aura (the energy field of protection surrounding the physical body).

Basic self. The lowest of the three selves. Has responsibility for the bodily functions, maintains habits and the psychic centers of the body, preserves the body. Also known as the lower self.

Causal realm. The realm above the astral. The realm of emotions, where the seeds of karma are kept. Intertwines with the physical realm as a vibratory rate.

Christ Consciousness. A universal consciousness of pure Spirit that exists within each person through the Soul. A Christ Consciousness is on each realm.

Conscious self. The second of the three selves. The self reading this and making conscious choices. The one that comes in as a *tabula rasa*.

Cosmic mirror. The mirror at the top of the void, which is at the top of the etheric realm, just below the Soul realm.

Etheric realm. The realm above the mental realm and below the Soul realm. The void and the cosmic mirror are at the top of the etheric realm.

Free choice. Exercised after incarnating. Reflects cooperation with or avoidance of the divine karmic path.

Free will. Used before incarnating. Determines the divine karmic path for that lifetime.

Hell. A state of negative consciousness; not a physically located place.

Hierarchy. *See* **Spiritual hierarchy.**

High self. The highest of the three selves. The self that functions as a spiritual guardian, offering the experiences that are for the person's highest good. Has knowledge of the life destiny agreed upon before embodiment, and holds to the divine agreement.

HU. A tone that is an ancient name/sound of the supreme God.

Human. Another way of saying "God-man. " Implies that each person has the essence of God within (as the Soul).

I AM. A synonym for the Soul.

Initiation. A Sound Current initiation connects a person to the Sound Current of God, the spiritual energy on which a person returns to the heart of God.

Initiatory tone. A tone given to an initiate in a Sound Current initiation. The name of the Lord of the realm into which the person is being initiated.

Innerphasing. An MSIA service. A technique designed to assist a person in changing habit patterns and programming in new, desirable responses by working directly with the basic self and its levels of responsibility.

Inner realm. One of the various realms of Spirit other than the physical realm.

Jehovah. Another name for the Lord of the causal realm. The God of the Old Testament.

Kal Niranjan. The Lord of negative creation. The spiritual name of the Kal power. *See also* **Kal power.**

Kal power. The power of the Lord of all the negative realms. Has authority over the physical realm.

Karma. The responsibility of each person for their actions. Cause and effect. Based on the concept that as you sow, so you reap.

Karmic board. A spiritual group of adepts (masters) who consult the akashic records and meet with a being before embodiment to assist in the planning of that being's spiritual journey.

Light. The energy of Spirit that pervades all levels of consciousness. The highest spiritual Light has its source in the Soul realm and above.

Light columns. Spiritual energy placed on/in a physical site by the Mystical Traveler, initiates, and ministers in MSIA.

Lucifer. A name sometimes given to the Kal power.

Magnetic Light. The Light of God that functions in the negative realms.

Meditation. Can be a passive process of attempting to empty the mind of all thought and feeling. In MSIA can also be used to mean guided meditation, an active process.

Mental realm. The realm above the causal. Relates to the mind. Intertwines with the physical as a vibratory rate.

Movement of Spiritual Inner Awareness (MSIA). An organization whose major focus is to bring people into an awareness of Soul transcendence. John-Roger is its founder and current spiritual advisor.

Mystical Traveler Consciousness. An energy from the highest source of Light and Sound whose spiritual directive is awakening Souls and guiding them back to the heart of God. Also called the Traveler.

Negative realms. The five lower realms, namely, the physical, astral, causal, mental, and etheric realms. *See also* **Positive realms.**

Ocean of Love and Mercy. A synonym for Spirit.

Physical realm. The negative realm in which a person lives while in the physical body.

Positive realms. The Soul realm and levels above. *See also* **Negative realms.**

Realms. Vibratory rates of existence.

Rukmini canal. An opening in the void at the top of the etheric realm through which a person moves in consciousness into the Soul realm.

St. Peter. The gatekeeper who checks a person's worthiness to enter the Soul realm. Resides in the astral realm. Also known as Yama, the angel of death. (Not the biblical Peter.)

Satan. A name sometimes given to the Kal power.

Satsang. Being in the presence of a spiritual teacher or guide who offers the teachings of Spirit. Communion with Spirit through a spiritual energy. May take place in the physical presence of such a being or in a gathering to view a video presentation or listen to an audio seminar.

Seminars. In MSIA this refers to the Mystical Traveler's teachings offered in live and recorded seminars from throughout the world. (Available on video or audio cassette from MSIA headquarters in Los Angeles.)

S.e.'s. *See* **Spiritual exercises.**

Soul. An extension of God individualized within the human being. The essence of human existence, forever connected to God.

Soul Awareness Discourses. Monthly publications offering the Mystical Traveler's teachings. Written by John-Roger and published by MSIA. One of the ways the Mystical Traveler works with people. Required study for initiation into the Sound Current.

Soul Awareness Tapes (SAT). Audiotape seminars by John-Roger, released by MSIA for further study of the Mystical Traveler's teachings. One of the ways the Mystical Traveler works with people.

Soul realm. The first of the positive realms and the true home of the Soul. The first level where the Soul is consciously aware of its true nature, its pure beingness, its oneness with God.

Soul transcendence. The process of moving the consciousness out of the physical body and conventional conditioning, above the negative realms, and into the Soul realm.

Soul travel. Traveling in Spirit to other realms of consciousness. Sometimes known as out-of-body experiences. This can be done in your own personal realms or in the outer realms.

Sound Current. The audible energy that flows from the God-source throughout all levels. Referred to in the Bible as "the Word."

Spirit. The pure essence of creation. Infinite and eternal.

Spiritual exercises (s.e.'s). The primary process permitting the Mystical Traveler to work with a being in the higher realms, in Soul transcendence. An active technique of bypassing the mind and emotions by chanting a tone (Ani-Hu, HU, or an initiatory tone) that connects one to the Sound Current.

Spiritual hierarchy. The spiritual forces that guide the earth plane. Works under the Logos or God of the planet.

Veil of forgetfulness. That process by which information about the divine plan and previous ernbodiments is not revealed, permitting the person to newly experience the teachings and lessons offered and to make the free choices toward spiritual progression.

Void. Located at the top of the etheric realm. The cosmic-mirror is above the void, just below the Soul realm.

Yama. The angel of death. *See also* **St. Peter.**

Index

A

A + UL =H 2+ W, 61
Abundance, 63, 64, 69
Acceptance, 2, 38, 49, 61-2, 63, 64, 89, 93, 105
Action, 38, 73, 104, 105, 108
Adamic language, 20
Addictions, 8-9, 13, 25, 110
Akashic board. *See* Karmic board
Akashic records, 3
Akashic records, lords of. *See* Lords of karma
Alcoholics, 9
Allah, 42, 100
Angels, 101-2, 108
    See also Guardian angel group, Guardian angels
Ani-Hu, 27, 47
Ascended masters, 10, 66, 80
Astral body, 5, 35, 36
Astral initiation, 42
Astral mind, 36, 37
Astral realm, 10, 11, 35-8, 63, 74, 110,
    See also Summerland
Astral realm (color of), 55
Astral realm (description), 5, 35-8, 91
Astral realm (Light on), 84-5,
Astral realm, (Lord of), 27, 30, 35, 38
Astral realm (Sound Current on), 50, 110
Astral realm (spiritual hierarchy). *See* Spiritual
    hierarchy
Astrology, 15
Atman, 21
Attitude, 65, 68, 76

Attitude and altitude, 93
Aura balances, 16
Avatar, 65, 66
Awareness, 33, 38, 73, 78, 90, 91, 92, 95

B

Balance (technique), 61
Band of five, 59, 60, 63, 65, 66
Baruch Bashan (meaning), 109
Basic self, 12-6, 18, 33, 110
Basic self (description), 7, 12, 13, 16
Basic self (job), 12-6, 21
Basic self (work with), 13, 16, 54
Beauty, 63
Belief, 80
Beloved, 99, 104
Births, 5, 15, 78
Body, 5, 12, 18, 39, 85, 97, 110
Brahma, 29
Brotherhoods, 80
     See also Great White Brotherhood
Buddha, 29, 60, 65

C

Causal body, 5, 31, 36
Causal initiation, 80
Causal realm, 10, 30-4, 37, 38, 60, 110
Causal realm (color of), 55, 110
Causal realm (description), 5
Causal realm (Light on), 84-5
Causal realm (Lord of), 30
Causal realm (nine aspects of planet Earth), 63-4
Causal realm (Sound Current on), 50, 110
Cause and effect, 30, 75

D

Daydreaming, 37-8
Death, 1, 17, 57, 58, 78
Demons, 73
Destiny, 17-9, 57, 59, 71
      See also Reembodiment (plan for)
Detachment, 25
Devil, 72, 73, 74-5
      See also Kal power
Disciples of Jesus, 55, 79
Discipline, 54
Discourses. *See* Soul Awareness Discourses
Divine degree in management, 27, 28
Divine inheritance, 44, 64, 70
Divinity, 103
Doctors, 93
DNA and RNA programming, 14, 31
Dreams, 37, 42

E

Earthbound spirits, 36
Ecology, physical, 87
Ecology, spiritual. *See* Spiritual ecology
Ego, 4, 8, 17, 70, 72, 89, 106
Ego (description), 2, 18-9
Ego (technique to handle), 18, 62, 68
Ego (value), 18
Ego trips, 90, 101, 102
Electromagnetic Light. *See* Magnetic Light
Emotionalizing, 97
Emotions, 13, 31-3, 60
Emotions (technique to handle), 26, 28, 32, 34, 35, 37
Emotive body. *See* Causal body
Energy (technique to use), 97-9
Enthusiasm, 89
Entity, disincarnate, 9-11, 36, 73

F

G

I

L

R

Tone. *See* initiatory tone
Traveler. *See* Mystical Traveler Consciousness
Truth, 88-90

U

Unconditional loving, 14, 44, 45, 57, 61-2, 63, 64, 67, 76-7,
        78, 81, 85, 101
Unconditional loving and Soul, 23, 99
Unconscious, 7, 8, 10, 11, 13, 25, 35, 110
Unconscious body, 35-6
Upper realms of Spirit. *See* Positive realms

V

Veil of forgetfulness, 4, 5, 15
Veil of forgetfulness (purpose), 17
Vishnu, 29
Void, 24, 26, 41, 74

WXYZ

Weight reduction, 28, 35
Will. *See* God's will
Willpower, 33
Withholding, 32, 33-4
Won't power, 33
Word, 50
Words (value), 52, 108
Worlds without end, 26
Yama, 74
        See also St. Peter
Zoroaster, 65

About the Author

A teacher and lecturer of international stature, John-Roger is an inspiration in the lives of many people around the world. For over four decades, his wisdom, humor, common sense and love have helped people to discover the Spirit within themselves and find health, peace, and prosperity.

With two co-authored books on the *New York Times* Bestseller List to his credit, and more than three dozen self-help books and audio albums, John-Roger offers extraordinary insights on a wide range of topics. He is the founder of the nondenominational Church of the Movement of Spiritual Inner Awareness (MSIA), which focuses on Soul Transcendence; founder and Chancellor of the University of Santa Monica; founder and President of Peace Theological Seminary & College of Philosophy; founder of Insight Seminars and founder and President of the Institute for Individual and World Peace.

John-Roger has given over 5,000 lectures and seminars worldwide, many of which are televised nationally on his cable program, "That Which Is," through the Network of Wisdoms. He has been a featured guest on "Larry King Live" and appears regularly on radio and television.

An educator and minister by profession, John-Roger continues to transform lives by educating people in the wisdom of the spiritual heart.

For more information about John-Roger, you may also visit: www.john-roger.org

Soul Awareness Discourses—
A Home Study Course for Your Spiritual Growth

The heart of John-Roger's teachings, Soul Awareness Discourses provide a structured and methodical approach to gaining greater awareness of ourselves and our relationship to the world and to God. Each year's study course contains twelve lessons, one for each month. Discourses offer a wealth of practical keys to more successful living. Even more, they provide keys to the greater spiritual knowledge and awareness of the Soul.

$50 for the first year's subscription
To order call MSIA at 323-737-4055

Soul Awareness Tape (SAT) Series

This audio tape-a-month provides members with a new John-Roger talk every month on a variety of topics ranging from practical living to spiritual upliftment. In addition, member of the SAT club may purchase previous SAT releases.

$100 for a one-year subscription
To order call MSIA at 323-737-4055

New Day Herald

MSIA's own bi-monthly publication which contains articles by John-Roger and John Morton, as well as a comprehensive listing of MSIA events and activities around the world.

A one-year subscription is free upon request
To order call MSIA at 323-737-4055, or visit www.ndh.org

Loving Each Day

A daily e-mail message from MSIA that contains an uplifting quote or passage from John-Roger or John Morton, intended to inspire the reader and give them pause to reflect on the Spirit within. Loving Each Day is available in four languages—English, Spanish, French and Portuguese.

A subscription is available upon request.

To subscribe, please visit www.msia.org

To order any of these items, to learn about MSIA events in your local area, or to request a catalog for wider selection of study materials, please contact MSIA or visit our website.

Movement of Spiritual Inner Awareness (MSIA)®
P. O. Box 513935
Los Angeles, CA 90051-1935
323-737-4055
soul@msia.org   www.msia.org